THE RISE AND GWRYCH CASTLE
———— ABERGELE ————
North Wales

The Arms of Hesketh 1985 (Gwrych Castle)

Published in 1999 by Mark Baker
© Mark Baker 1999 (All Rights Reserved)
No part of this publication may be reproduced or transmitted in any form or by any means, electronic or mechanical, including photocopy, recording, or any information storage and retrieval system, without permission in writing from the publisher.

ISBN 0 9537440 0 0
Printed by Gwasg Helygain Ltd., Tel: 01745 - 331411

CONTENTS

INTRODUCTION

CHAPTER ONE
THE DREAM

CHAPTER TWO
PARK, GARDENS AND GATEHOUSES

CHAPTER THREE
THE DUNDONALDS

CHAPTER FOUR
INTERIOR TOUR
(How it was)

CHAPTER FIVE
MISCELLANEOUS VENTURES

CHAPTER SIX
AS I AM

CHAPTER SEVEN
EXTERIOR IN IT'S PRIME
Walking Guide
(As it was)

CHAPTER EIGHT
THE FUTURE
(An Evaluation)
and Responses

CONTACT ORGANISATIONS

ACKNOWLEDGMENTS

FOREWORD

Mark started this project when he was only eleven years old. From a fascination with history and castles, Mark decided to try and find out more about the panoramic Gwrych Castle.

Uncovering much more than he could have anticipated in the beginning, Mark found that he was not alone with the magnetism and passion that he felt for Gwrych. He is the President / Founder of our Society, ASFOG. At the request of our members it was also suggested that Mark should write this book.

Undaunted by the onset of an illness and the demands of schoolwork, Mark has steadfastly remained resolute in his cause.

I am greatly encouraged to see a young member of contemporary society showing dedication, inspiration to others and an ability to want to make a positive contribution to the future of Britain's Heritage.

With appreciation,

Margaret Lambert-Jones
Chair - ASFOG (A Society for the Friends of Gwrych)
October 1999

Gwrych Castle

"I see you set in the limestone,
Your towers standing strong.
The wind whistling through,
The rain hitting your stone.

I see you set in the limestone,
I go past and wonder.
Why does no one care?
Dear Gwrych I love you so."

by Mark Baker

(This poem was presented to HRH The Prince of Wales)

ABOUT THE AUTHOR

From the age of four, I have consistently enjoyed a general interest in British Heritage, history, historical buildings and architecture.

Much of my inspiration is encouraged through the work of HRH The Prince of Wales, whom I had the privilege of meeting in March 1999 when I briefed him on my work with Gwrych Castle.

As I recognise the importance of preserving our heritage for future generations, I would very much like to make a positive contribution to this worthy cause.

Thanks to the immense support given by so many towards my Gwrych Castle project, I hope that recognition will be afforded to the forlorn, yet magnificently stupendous Gwrych Castle.

This book will help to ensure that Gwrych and some of its memories remain encapsulated forever. Hoping you relax and travel back in time, basking in the former glory of Gwrych Castle in its prime. Looking positively at the prospect of change - I believe that we can make a difference.

Mark Baker
(Youngest) Honorary Life Member of SAVE Britain's Heritage, London. (1999)
Aged 14 Years

In loving memory of those who remain close to my heart
Maisie Getley, David Masterson & Derek Jones (Artist)
for their genuine encouragement and affection.

With thanks to Peggy & Dave Jones of Rhyl.
Love and thanks always to Mum, Dad, Nan, Grandad,
Eric and all of my family.

INTRODUCTION

Gwrych Castle, near Abergele, the most beautiful limestone castellated mansion. Lonely and uninhabited for the past decade and nestled in the hillside woods. Surrounded by superabundant greenery, which certainly adds a patina of age, Gwrych can claim to be Britain's most stupendous Edwardian Country House. A fairytale white Castle that stretches with its world famous eighteen embattled towers, waiting to be given a new and glorious life. Built by Lloyd Hesketh Bamford Hesketh and enlarged by his descendants, it is one of the first Gothic faux Castles to be created in Europe. Called a folly, unlike its counterparts of Penrhyn and Bodelwyddan or even Eastnor Castle, Gwrych was a blueprint for all the Victorian mock Castles along the North Wales coast. It is a romantic dream, once a luxurious residence for the ancient Heskeths who resided there. Allowed to decay and deteriorate, it is in danger of becoming no more than Grade One listed rubble! It's amazing interior, palacious park, gardens and exotic exterior are sadly neglected. In 1997, our Society A.S.F.O.G. ('**A Society For the Friends of Gwrych**'), was set up to help find ways for conservation and restoration. The aims and objectives of the Society have been extremely successful over the last three years. Achievements so far, include maintaining Gwrych Castle and grounds in the 'public eye'. Through the society's mailing list and the medium of National Organisations, T.V, Radio, and the Press, Gwrych Castle now has many friends including Members of Parliament and supporters of A.S.F.O.G., from all over the Globe.

"Gwrych Castle" Early Watercolour from 1831
(then in the County of Denbighshire)

So far, through continual monitoring, our group has been instrumental in over-seeing developments with the guidance of many National Organisations. The Society has approached the Local Authority who assisted with securing the building in conjunction with CADW (Welsh Heritage), in 1998.

Publishing our three monthly newsletters, regular committee meetings and contact with the Council has placed our Society in a prominent position within the local community, whilst the continual erosion of this Grade One listed building continues as a result of exposure to the elements. The Society aims to work towards trying to secure the building and help to get repairs to the roof, floor, windows and ceilings.

Interested individuals can write to me and we do hope to work with CADW, as they are now saying that this building warrants a Heritage Grant – A.S.F.O.G. would offer positive support in any possible way.

"Greetings from Abergele" Postcard from the 1970's

A.S.F.O.G. would like to help rescue, secure, repair and then assist with monitoring the future of this magnificent Grade One listed building.

Within this book I have endeavoured to incorporate a comprehensive appraisal of the history of Gwrych. This includes a summary of the individual rooms (including the treasures once housed there), precious memories of yesteryear, captivating the atmosphere of Gwrych's former glory.

The Castle should be saved! This book describes the unfolding history of Gwrych and then its sad decline, highlighting some of the problem areas and searching for solutions and answers.

Enjoy!

CHAPTER ONE
THE DREAM

Lloyd Hesketh Bamford-Hesketh was born on the 9th August 1788 and as a child he dreamed of building a Castle dedicated to his maternal ancestors, the Lloyds of Gwrych. From all of my research, the first "Lloyd" living on the site of Hen Wrych was David Lloyd, who was alive in 1608. The earliest ancestor was Cunedda Wledig, who possibly dates back to 800 A.D. Lloyd's paternal ancestors were the Ancient Heskeths and it was in the 18th century that Roger Hesketh of Rossall and North Meols, fathered (in addition to his two legitimate children) it is claimed, several illegitimate offsprings along the coasts of North Wales and Lancashire. Among them, it is believed, that Robert Hesketh of Upton, near Chester, who by an Act of Parliament, was obliged to change his name to Bamford, his mother's maiden name, although a subsequent Act permitted him to change it back to Hesketh. His son Robert Bamford-Hesketh married Frances Lloyd in 1787, daughter of Reverend John Lloyd and heiress of Hen Wrych (old Gwrych Estate) as it was called. When Robert Bamford-Hesketh died in 1816, the Estate passed to his eldest son Lloyd Hesketh Bamford-Hesketh.

The story of the Heskeths begins with Richard de Heskeyth, Lord of Heskeyth whose grandson was alive in 1271. It is claimed that the Heskeths obtained many of their lands by marriage with a wealthy Cheshire family that originated in Staffordshire and had considerable estates in Lancashire; they were known as the "Fighting Fittons." Mary Fitton, a Maid of Honour to Queen Elizabeth I and dismissed from Court, was doubtless the "Dark Lady" of Shakespeare's sonnets.

Early in the 14th century Heskeyth of Hesketh's great great grandson assumed the Arms of Fitton: ("arg on a bend sa. three garbs or"). When Lloyd Hesketh Bamford Hesketh's father died in 1814, he came into an immense fortune. He employed Charles Augustin Busby to do an initial design for a "gothic style" building with a central oblong block. The west end contained the State Apartments, and the east the Private. Connecting this was a large circular keep surrounded by a semi-curtain wall. Charles Augustin Busby was born in 1786 and he was the son of Dr Thomas Busby, a musician and writer. He became a pupil of D.A. Alexander from whom he learnt the skills not only of building but also of engineering, especially in the use of cast-iron for construction which was frequently used at Gwrych. At the same time he studied at the Royal Academy Schools, where he won a gold medal in 1807. His work was exhibited every year from 1801 to 1811 and in 1804 he became secretary to the London Architectural Society. Busby's design for Gwrych was exhibited at the Royal Academy in March 1814. The near collapse of his career occurred in 1816 when it is claimed a roof designed by him fell down and so he emigrated to North America where he settled in New York. In 1820, he returned to England where in 1823, together with Amon Henry Wilds, he designed the eastern parts of Brighton. He died on the 18th September at only 48, supposedly bankrupt.

Though Lloyd did not choose Gwrych's design it was, however, the basis for Thomas Rickman's plans of 1817. Rickman was only appointed to complete the cast iron windows, but he submitted his primary drawings and with Lloyd Hesketh Bamford Hesketh's ideas, began to obtain a full scheme. It was more compact and with massing more effective. Busby's Castle was designed to be lower down on the flat and much longer, making the house all on the same level. The foundation stone was laid on the 13th June 1819 and Rickman was still involved in some capacity in 1820. Some of Rickman's elements are included in the main block but they are mostly due to Hesketh. Lloyd also employed an American, called Mr Boston who installed a 40,000 ton ice house on the hillside concealed in a tower behind Gwrych. Thomas Rickman born the 8th June 1776, was the father of Thomas Miller Rickman. Rickman Senior who was in an architectural practice in Liverpool and had already published in its first form the results of his pioneering study of medieval architecture, re-issued in 1817 as 'An attempt to discriminate the styles of English architecture from the conquest to the dissolution'. This initiated the classification and nomenclature as 'Early English', 'Decorated' and 'Perpendicular', which are still in use today. Thomas Rickman and John Cragg of the Mersey Iron Foundry collaborated and built in Liverpool the remarkable cast-iron churches of St. George, Everton, 1812-14 and St. Michael-in-the-Hamlet, 1814-15. Rickman, when he worked solo, used Cragg's components for his gothic windows and other iron building requirements. Rickman died on the 4th January, 1841. The

Hesketh Tower was probably finished in 1822 and the Stable Block probably built at the same time. Work on the immense façade was carried on by Hesketh and completed by 1853. Nearly all of the windows in the Castle are cast iron and were made by the Mersey Iron Foundry. They include a three and four light perpendicular design, excellent six lighters and all included transoms pierced with quatrefoils.

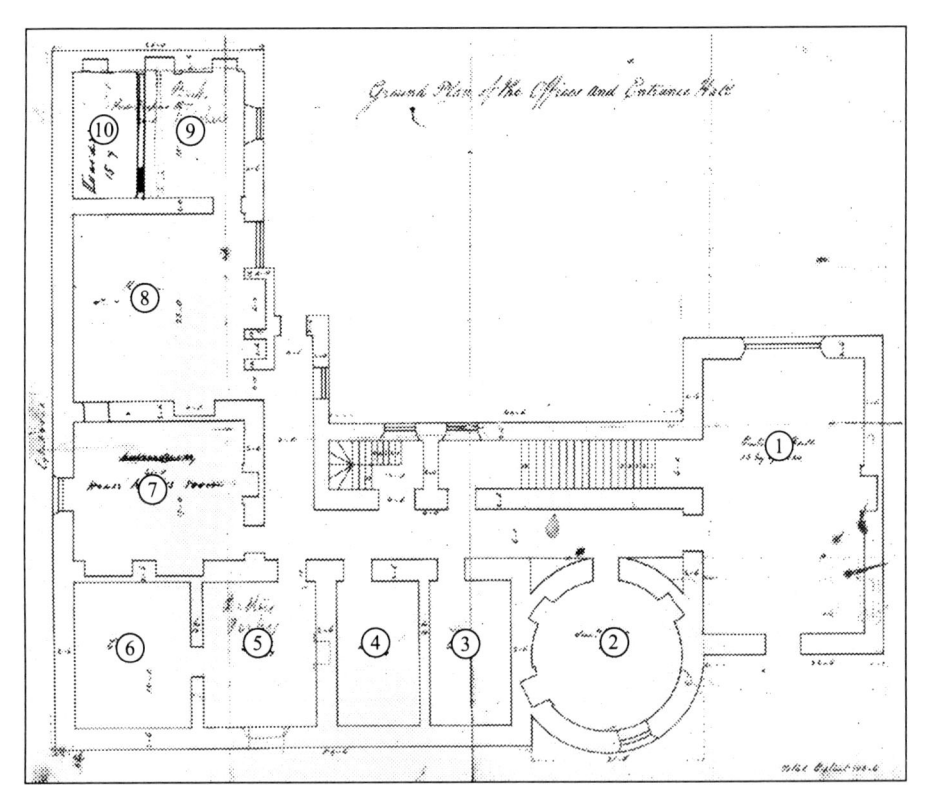

Basement Plan - 1820
by kind permission of the National Library of Wales

1	Mens Room	6	Butler's bedroom
2	Servants Hall	7	House Keeper's Room
3	Wine Cellar	8	Kitchen
4	Cellar	9	Back Kitchen
5	Butler's Pantry	10	Larder

The Duchess of Kent and her daughter Princess Victoria (later Queen) visited Gwrych, staying there for one night in 1832 and together with their company, occupied the West and Central Wings of the Castle. After returning from her tour of Anglesey, the Princess spent her next night at Kinmel Hall.

Another architect involved was Welch, who was already working at the Castle. Hesketh had the idea of an Estate Inn and designs were submitted by Welch but were rejected. The Inn would have been quite large, having two levels including the basement, various bars and numerous bedrooms. John Welch was brother of Edward Welch and was born in Overton, Flintshire on the 7th May 1810. He practised on the Isle of Man from

1830 in partnership with John Moore, a builders merchant, who also possibly published a book called 'Six days tour through the Isle of Man' in 1836. Welch then moved his practice to St. Asaph in 1839 and carried out some minor work at the Castle. He later moved to Preston where he died in 1855. For more important works Henry Kennedy was employed and the first sketches were made in March and April 1845. The foundation stone was laid on the 17th March 1846. In 1845-46 Kennedy made extensive alterations on the east side of the Castle – and all of the top storey of the east front was built as bedrooms of which the southern were Lloyd's and the northern were Lady Emily's in 1856. He also built a new staircase in the internal angle of the north and east ranges. This staircase was originally on five levels, tiered and took up only a quarter of the existing staircase, but Kennedy extended this further, adding the first and second Picture Galleries.

Henry continued the axis of his 1845/6 bedroom corridor by a means of a new flight of stone stairs and a porch which gave access to the Nant-y-Bella Drive. The lantern in the porch was placed here when the roof was being laid and it weighed a quarter of a ton being supported by cast iron joists. Henry Edward Kennedy worked from 1840-1897, the year in which he died. He was based in Bangor with Gustavas Hamilton O'Donoghue but by 1883 he was practising alone in Bangor, O'Donoghue having left for London.

Inner Hall - circa 1949
From the original design. The lanterns, woodwork and ceiling remained the same.
Note the catafalque on the right hand side of the room.

Original features of 1822 include the vaulted ceiling of the Inner Hall and the ceiling of the Outer Hall with its stone paved floor, the Regency Room's ceiling and all of the décor in the Music Room, the three pairs of mahogany doors, the Dining Room fireplace and the fittings of the Billiards Room. The brass balustrade surrounding the staircase is not of this time except for the brass gates which are from 1914; the original entrance being a single storey barbican style hall.

Interestingly, the Round Tower and Library Bay windows were original and so was nearly all of the heraldic stained glass which was designed by Lloyd and Rickman, with some by John Cragg. The Regency Room section and the two storeys above it are from Rickman's era and Kennedy's bedroom axis. Most of the surrounding façades are original except for the East lawn summer house, which was added in the 1870's.

Tapestry Sample made by Emma Williams and Lady Emily in 1844
Photo Courtesy of Rosemary A. Robinson (ancestor of Emma Williams)

After Lloyd Hesketh Bamford Hesketh inherited the Gwrych Estate, he married Lady Emily Esther Ann Lygon, youngest daughter of the 1st Earl of Beauchamp. They were married on the 28th October 1825 and moved into the spacious apartments of Gwrych where they had three children. Lady Emily's contribution was her tower which was built overlooking Tan-yr-Ogo. It was said to have been built for her and her children so that they could 'take the airs' and paint.

Here is a poem especially written by Lady Emily about the surrounding landscape viewed from the tower:

> *"Enchanting site! hence every rural sweet,*
> *And every natural charm to meet.*
> *Hence to the eye the landscape opens wide!*
> *The dancing spirits roll a quicker tide.*
> *Around new objects promp th' excursive lay:*
> *The gentle winding stream, the meadows gay;*
> *The smiling village sunk in leafy shades,*
> *That just unfolds its low through the glades;*
> *The splendid seat, the tower, the shining spire,*
> *And hills that catch the sun's departing fire."*

An inscription which can be found on Lady Emily's Tower reads 'The sea He has and He made it, the dry land He made' Psalm 95 Verse 5. This could refer to the spectacular views afforded from the tower.

Marble Staircase in the 1940's

Notice the large lantern, balustrade and superb tiling on the floor, which were of the original design.

When Lloyd Hesketh Bamford-Hesketh died in 1861 the Castle passed to his eldest son Robert Bamford-Hesketh. He was born in June 1826 and married Ellen Jones-Bateman of Pentre Mawr, Abergele in 1851. From most of the history relating to Gwrych, it is said that Robert did little if anything to the building, but it is also said that Lloyd Hesketh Bamford-Hesketh did not build the Castle's Marble Staircase; why should he want to so soon after Kennedy's magnificent staircase of the 1840's? It would be a waste of his resources, so it was in 1914 when Winifred Bamford Hesketh (his daughter) made most of the major renovations. I maintain that possibly Robert built the Marble Stairs. The staircase was a cascade of fifty-two marble steps, with three flights, the second of which leads to the first and second Picture Galleries and the third leads to Nant-y-Bella Porch. This delicate brass balustrade was not an original of 1822 and that is why it was mistaken to be of the same date as Kennedy's stairs. Notably, the balustrade of this construction was of a gothic wood design. The designer and exact date of the Marble Staircase has been lost in the mists of time but I can say it is of Italian design and origin, although it is said to resemble the one found in the Grand Hotel in Cairo.

Robert's main interests were with the Estate and the people of Llanddulas. Lloyd Hesketh Bamford-Hesketh was a benefactor of Abergele and he gave a memorial window to St. Michael's, (designer unknown). A Tablet in this Church is a memorial to the Hesketh family of Gwrych; it is half empty because Lloyd probably thought and wished that the Heskeths would be there for many generations after he died. But this was not to be, for 64 years later the 12th Earl of Dundonald moved out and that was the last time it was used as a home for the Heskeths. The Heskeths were famous for buying properties, Robert Bamford-Hesketh having a greater zest for this than his forefathers, making more than thirty transactions during his lifetime. As each transaction invariably contained several properties, the total in 1873 (twenty years before he died) was an estimated 3424 acres. He also owned numerous coal and mineral mines all over the North West. Robert was the Patron of George Edmund Street who was employed by Hesketh to build the large gothic school in Abergele, on Colwyn Bay Road in 1870. Street also built a first rate group of buildings consisting of a Church, Vicarage and School at Towyn in 1871-73. The Church has a 'saddleback tower' over the crossing and has excellent fittings (reredos by Earp, the East window and brass coronae by Hardman); the Vicarage is linked to the Church by a covered passageway. Seen in Abergele, as a trademark of Street's work, are the tri-coloured slates of the buildings in Towyn. Street had written a book on "Marble and Italian Architecture", possibly linking him with the staircase. The reason why the Heskeths "fell out" with Abergele occurred was possibly because when the family were not in residence, it was decided to install a Church organ at St.Michael's, but to make space for this the Hesketh pew had to be dismantled. Perhaps the family were not informed beforehand but when they became fully aware of their loss, they were furious and immediately transferred their religious observances to St. Cynbryds in Llanddulas. Again, Street was employed to design the Church on a lavish scale. The earlier Church was depicted as a plain stone building with a slate roof. Comprising of a nave and a north transept, it was smaller and to the south of the new Church, Lloyd Hesketh Bamford-Hesketh had actually repaired the north transept in 1841. George Edmund Street was born at Woodford, London, on the 20th June 1824 and went to Collegiate School, Camberwell. Articled to Gwen Browne Cartere of Winchester, from 1841, in the office of Sir George Gilbert Scott from 1844 to 1849, his practice began at Wantage in 1848. He moved to London in 1856 and his main office from this time until 1863 was at 33 Montague Place, until 1870 when he moved to 5 Russell Square. In 1868 he designed the London Law Courts and was the architect to the Dioceses of Oxford, York, Ripon and Winchester. By 1859, Street was awarded a FRIBA and a PRIBA in 1881. A Royal Gold Medal was also given in 1874; ARA 1866; RA 1871; FSA 1853 and a RA Professor of Architecture in 1880. His father was Arthur Edmund Street who is buried at Westminster Abbey. This very learned man published four books. Brick and Marble Architecture in Italy, 1855; The Cathedral of the Holy Trinity, commonly called Christ Church Cathedral, Dublin. An account of the restoration of the fabric, 1882; also The New Law Courts, 1864. He also published some accounts of Gothic Architecture in Spain in 1865 and he died at Cavendish Place, London on the 18th of December 1881.

Discovered in the Castle was an old contemporary newspaper of 1868, detailing the laying of the foundation stone for St. Cynbryds. "On Thursday 2nd July 1868 the foundation stone was laid by Mrs Ellen Hesketh and the youthful heiress of the massive fortunes of Gwrych, Miss Winifred Hesketh". Robert also installed a small two manual organ by Hill in 1869. In 1870, Robert also donated an alabaster and marble altar neredo for St. Asaph Cathedral which was being restored by Sir George Gilbert Scott. It depicts Christ's journey to Calvary. Hesketh was buried in a position near to the new Church, when he died on 29th April 1894. The Castle passed onto his only surviving daughter Winifred and when Ellen died in 1903, she was buried next to her husband in the grounds of the Church she had blessed.

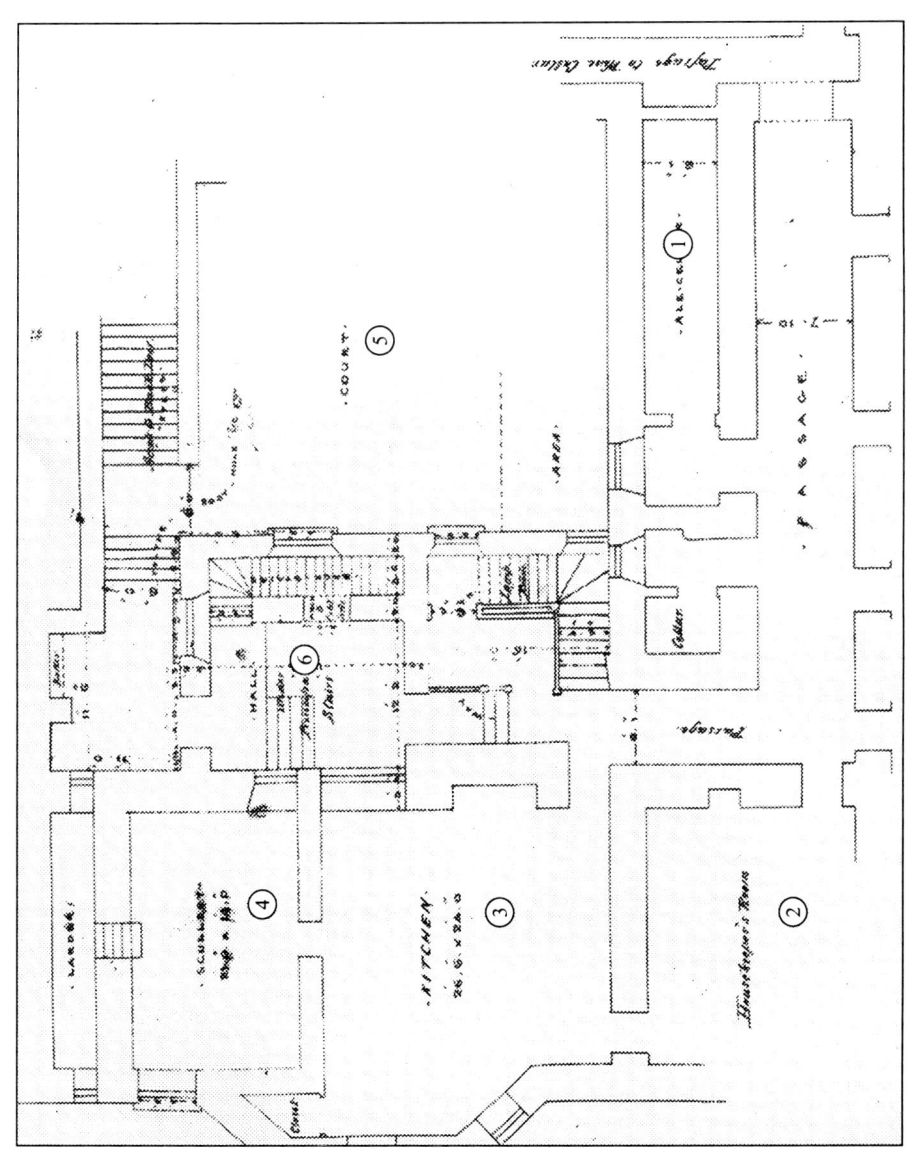

Basement Plan - 1845
by kind permission of the National Library of Wales

1. Ale Cellar
2. House Keeper's Room
3. Kitchen
4. Scullery
5. Kitchen Court
6. Hall below "Kennedy's Stairs"

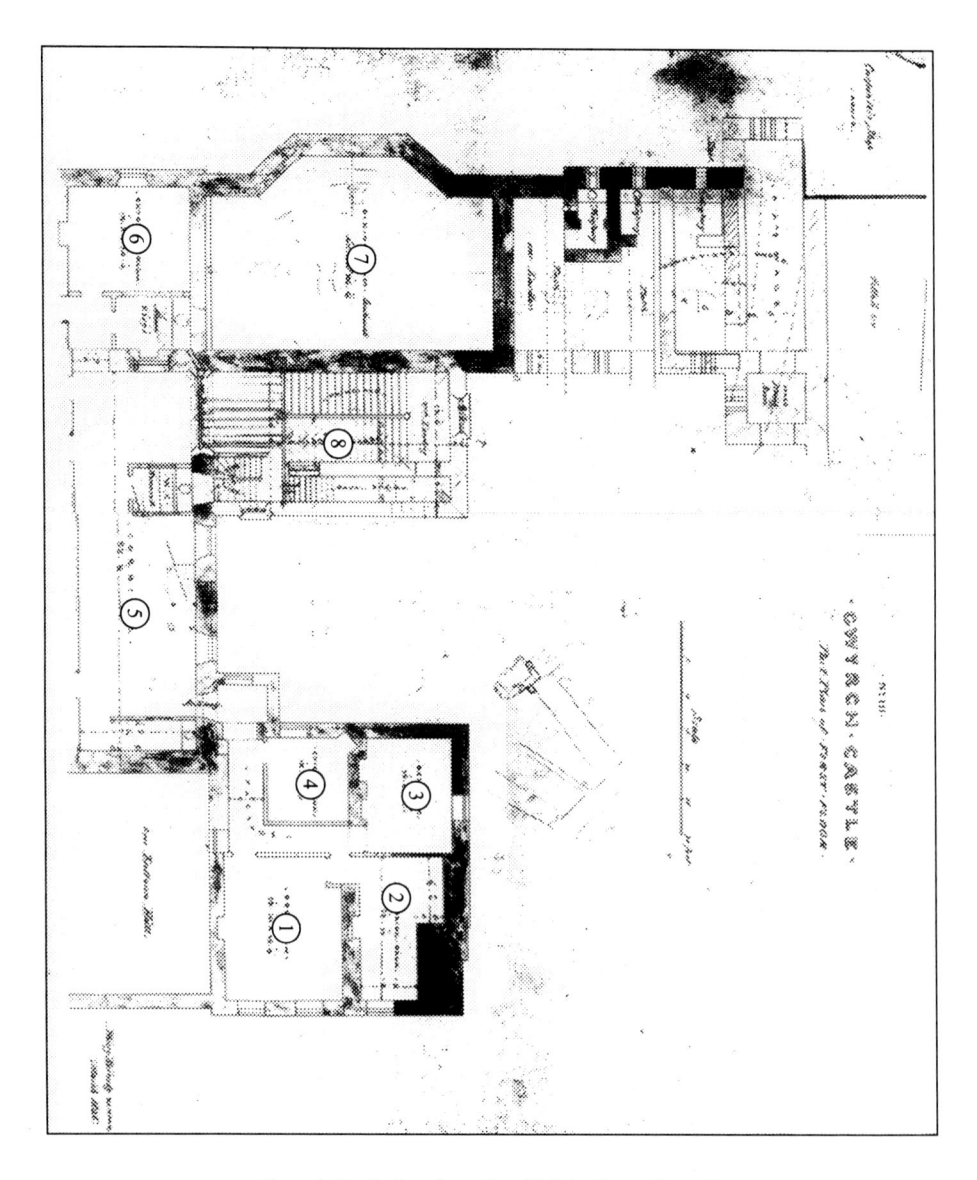

*Gwrych Castle first floor plan 1845 by Henry Kennedy
by kind permission of the National Library of Wales*

1	The Red Bedroom	5	Picture Gallery
2	West Tower Bedroom	6	Rhuddlan Room
3	Chintz Dressing Room	7	Upper Part of Dining Room (Ceiling)
4	Chintz Bedroom	8	Kennedy's Staircase

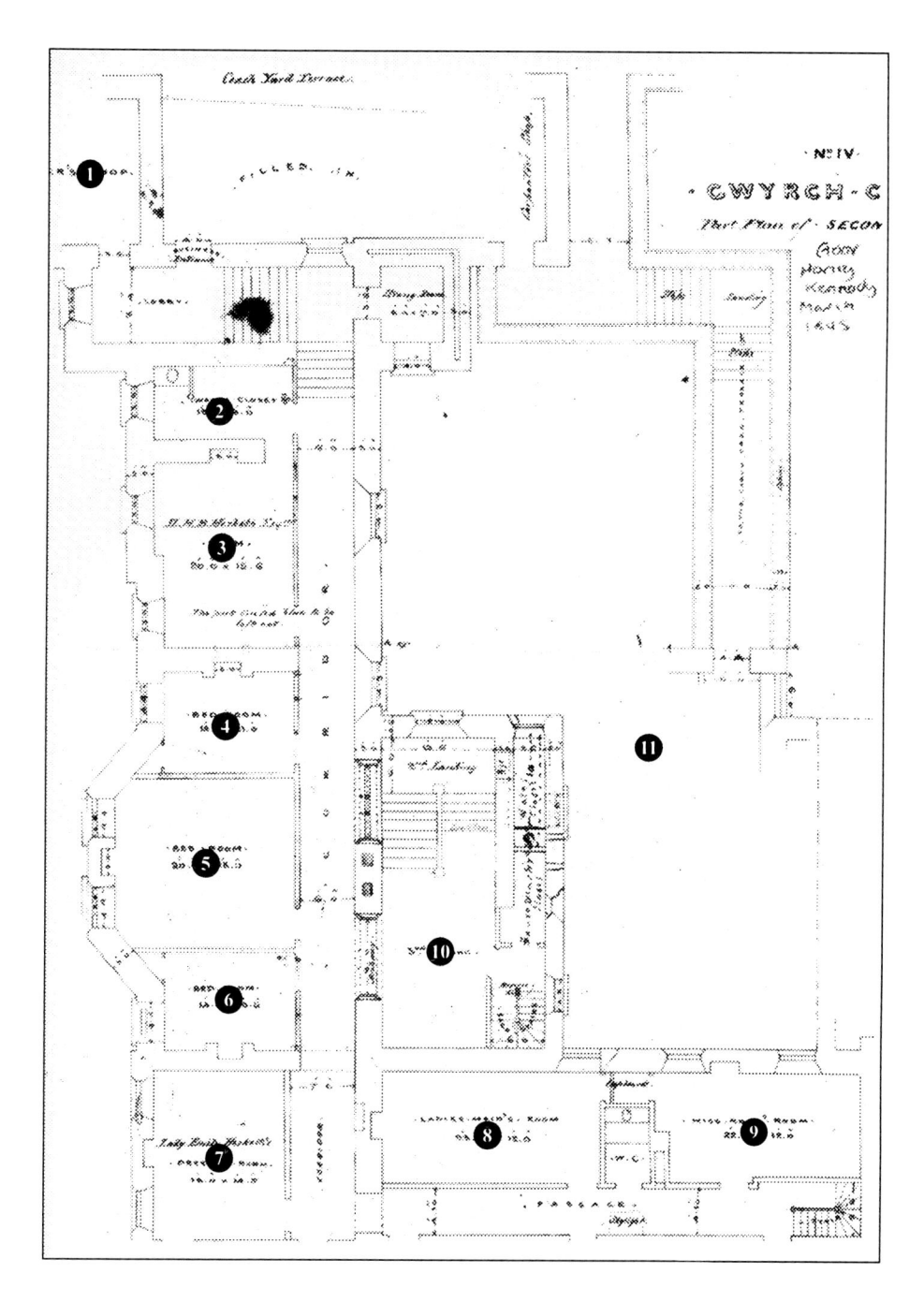

*Second Floor Plan March 1845 by Henry Kennedy
by kind permission of The National Library of Wales*

Gwrych in the 1880's

(notice the Barbican like Entrance Hall)

Key to plan on previous page:

1	Oak Room (Chapel)	6	Bedroom
2	Lloyd Hesketh Bamford-Hesketh's Dressing Room	7	Lady Emily's Room
3	Lloyd Hesketh Bamford-Hesketh's Bedroom	8	Ladies Maid's Room
4	Bedroom	9	Miss Ross's Room (Housekeeper)
5	Bedroom	10	Kennedy Staircase
		11	Kitchen Court

CHAPTER TWO
THE PARK, GARDENS AND GATEHOUSES

The park of five hundred acres is enclosed by a high wall made out of Llanddulas limestone. Huge meadows, rock outcrops and caverns, make the beautiful park worthy of its Grade II listed status. Gwrych Estate is one of the last intact parks in Wales which still has a complete boundary wall, gatehouses and the house at its centre. Starting from the western part of the park nearest to Llanddulas, is the mountain Cefn-yr-Ogof. The caves, formed by the sea, contain many fossils and are extensive. Below them is Tan-yr-Ogo named "the thermopylae of Wales". It was the scene of many fierce battles between the Welsh, Saxon and Norman invaders. The field, Cae Gerail (Field of Corpses) nearby once contained a small house called Tan-yr-Ogo Bella, whose stone was later used to build Tan-yr-Ogo gatehouse and to reinforce the old coach highway which ran along the base of the hill towards the direction of the Castle. In the 1820's the area was densely populated with all manner of trees, although only in certain parts because of the outcrops. The three main woods are the Great Castle Wood, the central "Hesketh Wood" and the easterly Blackthorn Covert; the woods are still said to be filled with deer, wood pigeons, pheasants, hawks, eagles, black, brown and white rabbits. Mineral mines were opened by the Romans and the stairs to the mines are named the "Roman Steps" but are not of that era, they were probably carved in the early 19th century. Lloyd Hesketh Bamford-Hesketh reopened the mines and eventually used the lead for the Castle. The Countess sold the mines and Quarries in 1919 and the woods, which were subsequently leased for 999 years in 1951 to the Forestry Commission by the Earl of Dundonald, remain very prominent in the coastal landscape. Great Wood rises to 650 feet on its south western boundary. At the Llanddulas end of the wood are the limestone cliffs and caves which form part of the Rhyd-y-Foel Site of Special Scientific Interest (SSSI). Areas of beech, oak and sycamore form part of the SSSI, the specific interest here is botanical and entomological. The site is designated due to the considerable range of interesting plant communities in a relatively small area. A cliff face supports various grasslands and tree species with woodland dominating the calcareous heaths on deeper drift soils. This area also supports a rich butterfly fauna. Lady Emily's Tower situated on a rocky outcrop is surrounded by trees and within the wooded hillside are the remains of a derelict cottage of which only one wall remains. The Hesketh Wood is filled with an amazing variety of trees, a multitude of firs, pine, larch and many oriental maples, hazels and cherries. Every season displays individual natural beauty, which is a pleasure to see.

Abergele Gates - 1950's

Blackthorn Covert also contains features of the old estate; there are at least two stone staircases which may have been part of an internal network of paths constructed to enable the estate owner to enjoy the woods without difficulty. Sections of the pathways still have dry stone retaining walls and near one of the staircases are the remnants of what appears to be an old water pump with the name "Francis Morton's Patent Liverpool". Beech, Scots pine, oak and Corsican pine are features of this wood. Fields below the Castle and woods were once landscaped into a beautiful park, deer roamed the lower paddocks and were hunted by the Castle family. The eastern part of the park is now used by the golf course. Ever expanding with superb views, the golf course now takes over half of the northern part of the park. The western end near Tan-yr-Ogo really shows off the rugged and romantic landscape, which was the park of Lloyd's dream. Behind the woods is the upper park, but just as seductive. The many woodland walks up to the park take you past hillside streams and superabundant greenery and glens; the upper park takes you round old mine shafts and up to the summit of Cefn-yr-Ogof. At Llanddulas is the old quarry which supplied Lloyd with his invaluable limestone for his luxurious Regency Mansion. Gwrych Castle gardens were mainly on the east lawn. The high path above the lawn contained the hillside rockery and the cottage garden. Clematis, fuchsias, irises, lavender, lillies and lobelias were the main features of the base of the south border.

Abergele Gatelodge (Kings Gate) and Tan-y-Gopa Road in the 1900's

The cottage garden was situated in an ingle nook between the old oaks and was filled with foxgloves, roses, lily of the valley and solomon's seal, which made this garden one of the most enchanting with interlocking staircases, hidden corners and wondrous grottos. Huge herbaceous borders, often extensive and very beautiful, could be seen all over the Castle. Gwrych's glasshouse on the east lawn had been originally the site of the formal garden, although later replaced by the new conservatory. Cotoneaster hedges and geraniums were moved to different parts of the Castle and the glasshouse, entered by a terrace to the south, it was guarded by a pair of huge Grecian urns. The huge conservatory was filled with hundreds of geraniums, carefully tended by Mr Reid, the Castle's Head Gardener at this time. Much of the old glasshouse became dilapidated in the late 1920's when the 12th Earl left Gwrych to live at Loch Nell Castle. By the 1950's the building had totally been dismantled except for the north wall which contained one of Rickman's six lighters and a small tower along with a fireplace and basement, which was used to heat the conservatory in winter. This was also used as a private retreat for the gardeners.

Tan-yr-Ogo Lodge in the 1950's

The 1970's and 80's saw the old formal gardens and glasshouse used as a jousting court; the decking for the spectators replaced the urns and the old terrace. All of the gardens were terraced and provided magnificent views over the Irish Sea and the so called "Bay of Naples". The central courtyard was nicknamed the "Kitchen Court" because it gave access to the servants' quarters and to the kitchens. It mainly served as a herb garden and had a small vegetable patch which was frequently used for all of those stately banquets which were put on by the Castle family. Another part of the Estate was Gopa Wood, which was to the east of Blackthorn Covert and contained much of the wood used for the heating at Gwrych. The Estates in North Wales covered land as far away as Colwyn Bay in the west, Prestatyn in the east and Denbigh in the south; the Heskeths also owned family Estates in the North West and the central parts of England.

Starting off with Mountain Lodge which guarded the southern entrance to Gopa Wood, is a small lodge with beautiful views. Although not really connected to Gwrych it was built by Lloyd Hesketh Bamford-Hesketh. North of this is Nant-y-Bella Lodge, which gave private access to the back of the Castle from Tan-y-Gopa Road. Although it had alterations from John Welch in 1842, it still retains Lloyd's original concepts and the Countess also carried out alterations on Nant y Bella when she extended the living quarters in 1912. The gatelodge is comprised of local limestone rubble and consists of a main storied section with a squat cylindrical tower; these are situated to the left and right of the driveway to the Castle. In the main part there is a square tower with crenellated battlements and a tall circular watch tower attached to the north front. The latter has a double corbelled upper stage, in imitation of machicolations and a shallow, conical slate roof with a small brown brick chimney to the rear. There is a pointed arched window to the front with a cusped, cast-iron frame to Rickman's design and a similar window to the inner return of the main tower, with a Tudor arched entrance below.

Detail of Nant-y-Bella Lodge

A later boundary wall made of rubble in the 1830's adjoins the watch tower to the south and a modern storied extension joins the rear of the main block. The cylindrical tower to the north has a corbelled upper section, though this lacks battlements. Two half round stone gate piers adjoin both this and the watch tower; sadly the gates are missing. Down the road towards Abergele, is the King's Lodge, or Abergele Lodge. The main entrance to Gwrych is through these gates, featuring a dramatic pair of huge drum towers with corbelled overhangings and a battlemented top, a single gothic arch gate over which is a shield depicting the Arms of Fitton. Behind this is a barbican and another arch gate which leads you into the Castle park. Along the park wall towards Llanddulas is Hen Wrych, the former ancient home of the Heskeths. The lodge consists of a twin arched entrance between flanking square battlemented towers of local limestone rubble and limestone dressings; the adjoining walls begin at the east end at a small round turret with a corbelled parapet. This is not shown on the Ordinance Survey map of 1873. The section of the wall between here and the gated entrance has a small blocked pointed arch doorway with a blocked slit-light, ten metres east. Beyond are the two four-centred arch gateways. These have dressed voussoirs and are set back between taller square towers with deeply corbelled parapets, including diagonal corbelling at the corners with a lower similar parapet over the gateways, the left hand of which leads up to Gwrych Castle, the other into the forecourt of Hen Wrych. Above the gateway is a centrally placed limestone shield with cast-iron rosettes. Contemporary plain 19th century half gates survive at both entrances.

Gwrych Castle pre 1912

The left tower is Gwrych Lodge House, having three small paned cast-iron windows to the rear (entrance front), four centred arches and voussoirs as before. There was an advanced storied entrance bay to the right, with a modern boarded door to a Tudor arched entrance and modern glazed porch. A 19th century chimney made of brick adjoins the corner of this.

The East and Front Lawn in the 1890's. In the background on the hillside is the water tower.

Interestingly, the rear of the right hand tower has a camber headed doorway and a four centred arch window opening. The cast-iron glazing by Rickman has been recently removed in the early part of 1997. Twenty metres to the west, the wall steps down at a masonry break where a square tower with corbelled but un-battlemented parapet abuts, flush with walls to the front. The wall steps down again beyond this to continue westwards to adjoin a further similar tower. This has been heightened and forms part of Nursery Cottage, a modern house built to the rear of and abutting the wall. Immediately left of this tower is a blocked small pointed-arched doorway. Further west is a broader entrance, now filled with breeze blocks, with another masonry break and a further stretch of crenellated wall terminating in a similar flush bastion at the western most corner of the walled gardens. A recent low roadside wall continues up to a broad gated entry to the former gardens. The gardens to the north are divided by similar crenellated stone walls and red brick walls are the backdrop to the gardens. Although the western most garden is almost square, the south wall has been removed and the west stone wall is buttressed. Inside is a transverse stone range of sheds with grouted slate roofs, chimney stacks and square headed openings. The next two gardens are trapezium shaped, the eastern of which includes a Dutch Barn and to the southeast of that, there is a long stone barn with central barn doors and slit ventilators. South of these is a red brick walled garden, which is rhomboid shaped and behind that is a stone wall which on its north side is a planted area. These gardens are screened from the drive to Gwrych by trees via a long straight lane, which is entered by a small barbican.

Gwrych Castle from the Hesketh Tower in the 1890's showing Hesketh Wood in the background.

The next lodge is really a collection of buildings, Tan-yr-Ogo being the largest and most dramatic of all the Castle's lodges. Impressively, the façade on the southern side of the A547 is the entrance gates to Gwrych Castle and behind them is the main lodge; across the road, Tan-yr-Ogo farm and hall. A medieval style gateway with large flanking drum towers in a symmetrical arrangement is the main entrance to the Castle and a large Tudor arched entrance is set centrally within a tall castellated wall, some 10 metres high and 30 metres wide. The battlements have large crenellations, with over sailing ramparts an imitation of machicolation. Those sections corresponding to the embrasures are deeper than those to the merlons and the former. Consisting of two on each side of the entrance, which contain recessed sandstone inscription tablets and commemorate various historical events which have taken place on this important strategic site.

The tablets were inscribed from left to right as follows:

1. Prior to the Norman conquest, Harold in his attempt to subjugate this part of the principality was engaged in battle by Gruffudd ap Llewelyn, Prince of North Wales, on the plain near Cefn Ogo. After a sanguinary battle in which he was defeated, he was driven back to Rhuddlan.

2. In the reign of William the Conqueror, Hugh Lupas passing through the defile on his march to invade the Isle of Anglesey, was attacked by an armed band of Welshmen who had been posted there to anticipate his progress and of whom, after an obstinate and protracted battle, eleven hundred were left dead on the spot.

3. In the reign of Henry II, Owen Gwynedd, Prince of North Wales, on his return from Flintshire, fortified himself in this pass when he gave battle to the forces of that Monarch and repulsed them with great slaughter. Having secured the important post he retreated to Pen-y-Parc in the adjoining Parish where he made headway against the English forces and effectively checked the further invasion of his dominions.

4. Near this pass, Richard II whom Percy, Earl of Northumberland had inveigled from Conwy Castle on his return from Ireland under the promise of an amicable interview with Bollingbroke, was surrounded by a military band bearing the Northumberland banner and conducted to Flint Castle by the Earl unto the power of the usurper, (later Henry IV), in 1399.

Flanking the entrance are stepped buttresses and towards the centre of the left wall section is a blocked arched entrance with advanced drum towers joined to the entrance wall by short embattled link sections. The upper stage of the tower is corbelled out and now has large crenellations. Adjoining the right hand drum tower to the right (west) is a lower wall section some 3.5 metres high, which continues westwards for some 42 metres. Here it terminates just around the corner at the junction of the Abergele Road with Rhyd-y-Foel Road in a small corbelled turret. The wall section itself is crenellated and has large projecting corbelled out merlons. Adjoining the left hand drum tower to the east, a similar wall runs eastwards for 35 metres where it joins a large unbattled drum tower with a corbelled upper stage. Leading southwards from this a plain wall which runs for 20 metres at a height of 3 metres, before turning at a right angle and continuing for the same distance at a height of 6 metres. The wall then turns south again and continues for 20 metres more, where it terminates in a large round tower corbelled as before and with a bartizan to the north. East of the roadside drum tower the wall steps down slightly and continues for another 8 metres where it turns a right angle and advances towards the road for a further 8 metres. At this point the wall turns eastwards once more and continues as before for some 15 metres; at the corner is a tall turret with a corbelled upper stage. Three metres to the left of this is a Tudor arched opening with a modern steel door. Some 6 metres beyond this the wall again turns at a right angle, terminating finally with another corner turret.

From here, a wall runs southwards in similar fashion for some 48 metres into the rising slope of the hill to terminate at a modern field gate. A modern barn backs onto a part of this. Behind the façade is Tan-yr-Ogo Lodge with an entrance gate with tall flanking square towers, having crenellated and corbelled battlements made of limestone rubble with dressings and a tall Tudor arched entrance with a corbelled storey above. This has six tall modern windows with plain glazing and a modern shingle hung rear. The towers had modern glazing to Tudor arched upper windows facing north. That to the right (west) had been extended westwards in the later 19th century, having two of Rickman's windows to the rear. Adjoining to the front are short stretches of link wall terminating in turrets with corbelled upper sections. The buildings mentioned so far are all Grade II listed, except for the Abergele gates and Mountain Lodge, which are not listed. Across from Tan-yr-Ogo gatehouse is Tan-yr-Ogo hall and farm. The hall was partly built by Lloyd and is built of local limestone rubble with Rickman's cast-iron windows and a slate roof. Although the farmhouse is much older than its counterparts, it is probably 18th century and has many old out-buildings. However similar to the hall, it has hardly any of Rickman's windows. Finally, the last lodge is Betws, one of the smallest, but its exterior is deceiving. The interior is a small house of only three or four rooms and the exterior shows a high corbelled wall and a high battlemented parapet. Nowadays, the lodge is a farm and has been extended to suit the demands of a modern working farm.

CHAPTER THREE
THE DUNDONALDS

Drawing Room in the 1890's (by kind permission of Denbighshire Record Office)

Winifred Bamford-Hesketh was born on 16th April 1859 in Torquay, Devon. In 1860, Lloyd Hesketh Bamford-Hesketh and Robert Bamford-Hesketh arranged with Thomas Barnes, 11th Earl of Dundonald for a marriage with his son, Douglas Mackinnon Baillie Hamilton, Lord Cochrane, with the Hesketh's Heiress Winifred. When Lloyd Hesketh Bamford-Hesketh died in 1861, the Estate passed to his son, Robert Bamford-Hesketh. As stated in chapter one, Winifred and her mother laid the foundation stone of St. Cynbryds in Llanddulas when she was nine years of age; at the same time she had a German Governess, Theresa Auhe of Prufaias, Berlin. I am not sure what relationship they had, but I know that Winifred could converse in German. Lloyd Hesketh Bamford-Hesketh was a strong and forceful character and he and his son were extremely intelligent; these characteristics shone through in Winifred. I have to wonder how she would have taken the arranged marriage, noting her strong character! She was brought up with her grandparents at Gwrych and grew very close to her grandmother, Lady Emily. I have found no evidence of Winifred meeting Lord Cochrane during their childhood, but when she was in her teens a meeting was arranged. On 18th September 1878 Lord Cochrane married Winifred at only nineteen and a trust fund was set up for them (records indicate that £2000 was taken out of the rents of the Estates in Cheshire and Lancashire each year). The wedding day was a great occasion for the people of Abergele who were always more than ready to make a celebration and this was, of course, a very special event and held locally as a public holiday. Two bands played – the Llanddulas Band at the Castle and the Denbigh Volunteer Band in the town. Church Bells rang, guns were fired and a mounted escort formed by the tenants of the Estate attended the bridal couple on their return from Llanddulas Church. The Arch Deacon of St. Asaph (Winifred's Uncle) officiated at the service, assisted by the Vicar of Llanddulas and the Vicar of Towyn. Hundreds of tenantry including the local population were entertained to tea at school rooms and village halls. In the evening, a public dinner was held for well-wishers at the Bee Hotel, High Street, Abergele, followed by a great ball. After her marriage to Douglas, Winifred then became Lady Cochrane. On 16th April 1880, Lady Winifred's 21st birthday, the money in the trust fund could now be accessed and a house in London was bought.

Conditions were laid down in the last will of Lloyd Hesketh Bamford-Hesketh and monitored by her father, Robert. On 14th May 1880, Grizel Winifred Louise Cochrane was born at St. George's Hospital, Hanover Square, London. Sadly on the 15th January 1885, Thomas Barnes, 11th Earl of Dundonald died, whereupon Douglas and Winifred became the 12th Earl and Countess of Dundonald. The couple had several children, Thomas Hesketh Douglas Blair, Lord Cochrane, born 21st February 1886 at St. George's, London; Jean Alice Elaine, born 27th November 1887 at Mayborne, London; Marjorie Gwendolen Elsie, born 18th December 1889 at Mayborne, and the youngest child, Douglas Robert Hesketh Roger, born 24th June 1893 at Gwrych. Twenty six days earlier Robert Bamford Hesketh, the Countess's father died on 29th April 1893. Winifred and her company went to the Castle at Christmas, Easter and two weeks in August; the rest of the time was spent in London or at Loch Nell Castle, in Argyll.

Stable Hill 1960's, the Stable Cafe sign is clearly visible. Remarkably Stable Hill had not changed much since being built.

The relief of Ladysmith and the Countess's temper are forever linked at Abergele in the name of Dundonald Avenue. "A deep and bitter feud has prevailed between the historic house of Gwrych and the town of Abergele for many years" (reported in the Abergele Visitor, 16th February 1900). That was just twelve days before the Earl ended the one hundred and thirty four day siege by the Boers. The people of North Wales were more concerned with the relief of Pensarn, a former independent township and beach resort linked to Abergele by a tree lined lane of great beauty. Also reported in the Visitor was "Every attempt to improve the town for visitors has met strong opposition from Mrs Ellen Bamford Hesketh and her daughter, the Countess of Dundonald". Gwrych Castle had opposed the Local Government Union of Abergele and Pensarn on the grounds of divide and rule and as the family owned nearly all the land they were in a powerful position. Abergele Urban Council wanted to buy a strip of land for a road parallel to Pensarn Lane (Dundonald Avenue), which would have to be left as a footpath without affecting the old trees, but after years of dispute, the Countess replied in January 1900, ordering the Council to abandon their plans. She emphasised her ultimatum by felling three trees, saying that the rest would follow if the Council would not surrender within forty eight hours, adding that there would be no negotiations. The Council did not back down and Winifred remained true to her word, felling every tree along the lane. It was and still is named Dundonald Avenue – in honour of the Earl's victory at Ladysmith, South Africa. The siege of Ladysmith was one of three sieges of the second Boer War, in which the Boer forces attempted to pen up their British opponents. An attempt to relieve the town was frustrated at the battle of 'Spion Kop' (January 1900), but General Sir Redvers Buller and the Earl of Dundonald led the cavalry in the successful siege of the 28th February 1900.

Returning from Ladysmith. The Earl and Countess of Dundonald on their procession through Abergele in November 1900
Courtesy of Mike Roberts

On the afternoon of 23th February the Earl's cavalry, well in advance of the main forces, were within six miles of Ladysmith. The Earl and his soldier/war correspondent Winston Churchill (later to be Prime Minister), accompanied by a few orderlies passed unnoticed by the Boer units and on lathered horses they received a rapturous welcome from a starving town. Immediately, the Earl sent a message to General Buller, giving his position. When word was sent to Britain of the relief of Ladysmith, the populace were extremely happy. Robert Jones, printer and editor of the Abergele 'Visitor' devoted his whole newsletter to the Earl and Ladysmith. Countess Winifred informed the town's leading figures that her hero husband was expected home at the end of November on the 3.10pm train. It was decided that a sword and an illuminated public address should be made. Three hundred pounds were given to Mr William Humphrey-Jones, Jeweller of Chapel Street; he was asked to design and supply the sword; the address was to be printed by Messrs Waterlow of London. Mr W Humphrey-Jones was helped by one of Birmingham's finest jewellery firms, Vaughtons Limited. When the great day arrived, the train promptly arrived on the be-flagged station. The Earl was greeted by the Countess and her mother, Mrs Hesketh who had arrived by landau. Next came the presentation to the Earl of leading Abergele citizens. Amidst cheers the horses were taken out of the shafts; one hundred sturdy local men replaced them before the procession was led by the 'H' Company Volunteer Battalion Royal Welsh Fusiliers Band. The Earl's carriage moved off, followed by the Abergele and Districts Committees. Excited crowds gathered and the whole town was be-flagged and decorated with triumphal arches; the first stop was at Street's school of 1869 where little Cissie Thomas of Chapel Street presented a bouquet to Mrs Ellen Bamford-Hesketh. A second stop was made at Glanaber where another bouquet of 'red, white and blue' flowers was presented to the Countess. The final destination was Gwrych Castle Park (now the Clubhouse of the golf course) where a platform was erected. Colonel and Mrs Cornwallis-West, the Bishop of Bangor, Mr Thomas Hughes, his wife and Lady Florentia Hughes of Kinmel Park awaited. The Colonel read out the address together with Mr Grabbe. He presented the sword (a normal cavalry sword) in lieu of the actual sword. In reply, The Earl of Dundonald said that he was overwhelmed by the warmth of his reception and gave a brief outline of his exploits as Commander of an irregular brigade. He was then accompanied by his Gwrych coachman Rumph and his valet Nichols who, dressed in khaki, sat on the box of the carriage. Waving his sword, the Earl said that he had received a true Celtic welcome and the ceremony ended at 4.30pm when the coach drew up at the Castle gates. In the town the revelry continued at the Bee Hotel. The Earl was later made Governor of Canada, a post which he held until 1904. (The actual sword currently remains at Lochnell Castle, home of the present Earl).

*Robert Davies, Chauffeur to the Countess (formerly of the Square in Llanddulas) Circa 1907
Courtesy of Roberta Penlington*

Winifred mainly brought her own staff from London to attend on her, but local staff were also brought in. The Countess had always shown readiness to support local charities and activities, she took a prominent role in various organisations, amongst which were the Church Defence Movements including the Primrose League. Her public work was not just confined to the district. Robert Davies who was the Countess's chauffeur was sent to London in the 1900's to learn to drive. When he returned, he taught Winifred to drive her car, or took her on short journeys through the country. The Countess also used to let visitors travel by horse and trap from Abergele gate to Tan-yr-Ogo gate via Gwrych Park at a small charge; the proceeds all went to charity.

Gwrych in the 1920's, with the panoramic woodlands behind the Castle.

Charles Ernest Elcock was born in Belfast in 1878 and he was educated at Bootham School, York. Attending Belfast Technical College from 1895-96 and the Belfast School of Art, he was articled to Messrs J.J.Phillips and Son from 1896-1901, later moving on to Lawson's Travelling Studentship. He then became an assistant to John James Burnet from 1901-05 and then onto Messrs Matear and Simon from 1905-06. Receiving an IRIBA in 1911 and a FRIBA in 1912, he commenced his independent practice in Colwyn Bay in 1906. In partnership with J.M.Porter from 1906-1912 and later with John Brooke in Manchester in 1912-14, he died in 1944 at the age of 66.

Around 1911, the Earl and Countess of Dundonald employed Charles Ernest Elcock to extend the northwest entrance of the main Castle (barbican-like) upwards, adding more rooms to the first and second floors with the original west wing behind it. Early on in 1912 building work started and the family commuted to London and also to Lochnell Castle in Scotland, the Earl's family Estate. The Countess decided that her new car needed a new garage and so Elcock designed that together with the Estate offices. All of this, together with the work on the main house, was finished in 1914. Elcock also refurbished some of the old interior and the huge Welsh vernacular fireplace which was decorated with the Arms of Fitton, dated 1914. Chandeliers which were present in most of the state rooms are of this time, except for the ceramic light in the Music Room. The original Dining Room of 1822 was very gothic with armour and tapestries, but Elcock's treatment was very classical. With a heavily ornamental two-tier ceiling with fruits and flowers on the two cornices, having two Corinthian columns propping up the window arches, the statues on the staircase of Apollo and Artemis (originally in the Oak Room and Old Chapel) together with the green marble dado are of the same time as Elcock. The window at the top of the stairs designed by Rickman was reinstated with glass designed by Elcock in 1914.

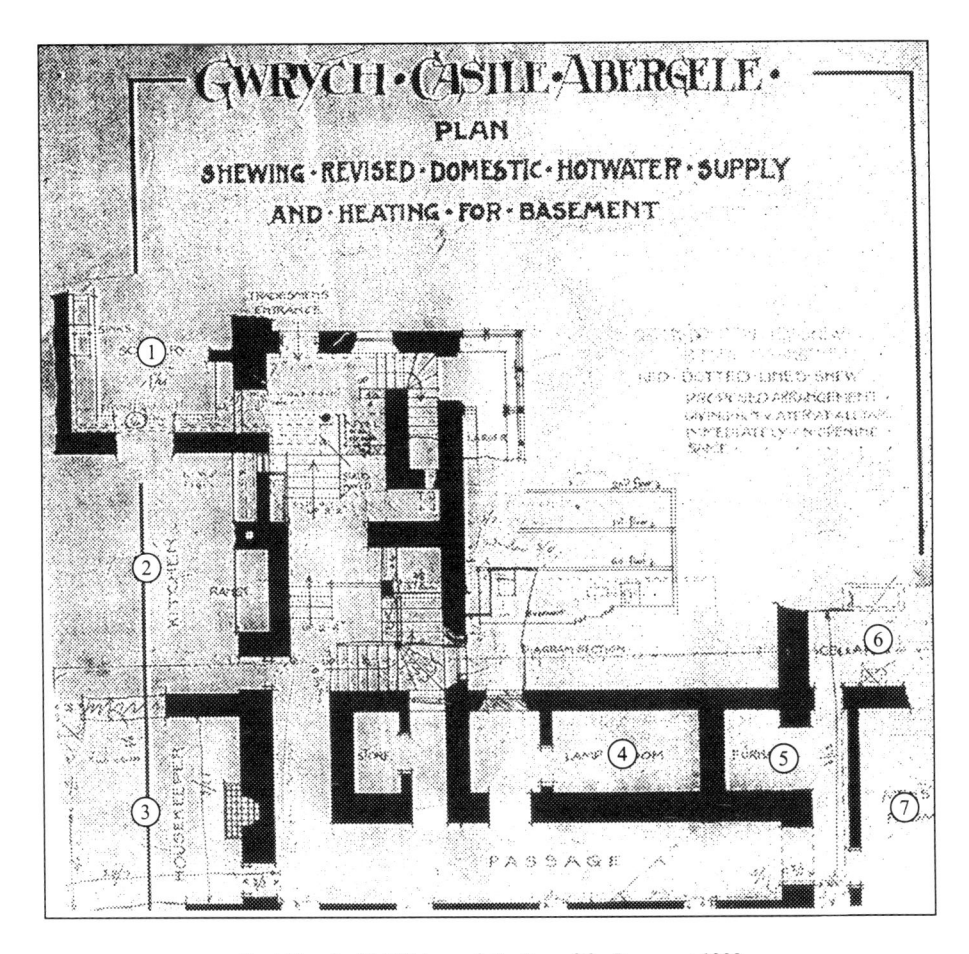

GWRYCH·CASTLE·ABERGELE·
PLAN
SHEWING·REVISED·DOMESTIC·HOTWATER·SUPPLY
AND·HEATING·FOR·BASEMENT

*Part Plan for Hot Water and Heating of the Basement 1909
by kind permission of Denbighshire Record Office*

1	Scullery	4	Lamp Room
2	Kitchen	5	Furnace
3	Housekeeper	6	Cellar
		7	Men's Room

In 1914, Dr A. Ely Edwards was the Bishop of St. Asaph. The Countess, who was a regular visitor to the Bishop's Palace, was rewarded by the Bishop who loaned his best Butler to Gwrych. If the situation had been suitable, the Butler, his wife and two daughters would have moved to Tan-yr-Ogo Hall. Although the Hall was too big, he occupied the Butler's apartments at Gwrych and so the rest of the family stayed at the Palace Lodge in St. Asaph. In August 1915, the two daughters went to see their father the Butler at the Castle. They arrived by horse and cart for the afternoon and had tea, then looked around. When they left at 4 p.m. they did not know that only an hour later, their father would be dead. Sadly, at only 42, the Butler had a massive stroke. The mother of the two girls left it to them to sort out the funeral arrangements because she was too grief-stricken to help; the Bishop sent a telegram to the family to halt the funeral until he returned to St. Asaph.

The Countess also commissioned the workers' cottages in Abergele, including those for her staff. When there was any serious illness, the Countess would donate soup to the families on the Gwrych Estate. David Jones of Llanddulas was very much overawed, having to wait in the Outer Hall of Gwrych, before returning home with his portion of soup. Mr Evans of Tan-yr-Ogo Farm was reported to have delivered a daily supply of fresh milk to the Castle. When the milk arrived late for the Countess's early morning tea, it was claimed that the Butler severely scolded Mr Evans!

It is well-known that the Countess during the Great War refurbished a house in London with over sixty beds for wounded soldiers and also supplied two field ambulances for France. The Earl, now a Major General, took a leading part in the war of 1914-18. It has already been mentioned earlier about Winifred's contributions during this time. In 1919, the Countess decided to sell some of the old buildings on her Estate and the Llanddulas limestone and mineral mines were sold to a company not unlike I.C.I. After the war the family made more frequent visits to London and on 16th January 1924 the Countess of Dundonald died there. All of the house was covered in black and the district went into mourning. One of her great friends, Lady Florentia Hughes of Kinmel Park, was a principal mourner. The Countess's body lay in state, like her predecessors, on the catafalque at the end of the Inner Hall. All of the Estate and her many friends and children were packed into St.Cynbryd's Church, Llanddulas. Lady Grizel Hamilton (title by marriage) led the service and her husband, by now 72, praised the Countess for her work during the war and for Llanddulas. Winifred was buried next to her mother and father, although her grandparents were both buried in St. Michaels churchyard in Abergele along with some of their children. The Earl and Countess chose not to be buried there. It is believed the money from the sale of 1919 went to a memorial cross designed by Harold Hughes of Bangor, in the style of the Lych Gate, which was erected in the centre of the Hesketh plot in St.Cynbryds Churchyard. For some unknown reason, it is claimed that the poor Earl was left out of the Countess's Will! Winifred also bequeathed money for Alms Houses which would be dedicated to her memory. Gwrych was willed to Prince George of Wales (later King George V). His Majesty was unable to accept the gift and by her further bequest, the Castle was sold. Half the proceeds went to the Church of Wales and the other half to the Order of St. John of Jerusalem. The Order then bought the Castle which was subsequently sold to the Earl who, it is believed, paid £70,000 for it.

The Countess Winifred Laying the Foundation Stone of the Church House in Llanddulas - 1910
Lady Grizel is to the left of the picture and Lady Jean is in front of her.
Courtesy of Idris Davies and Llanddulas Village Hall

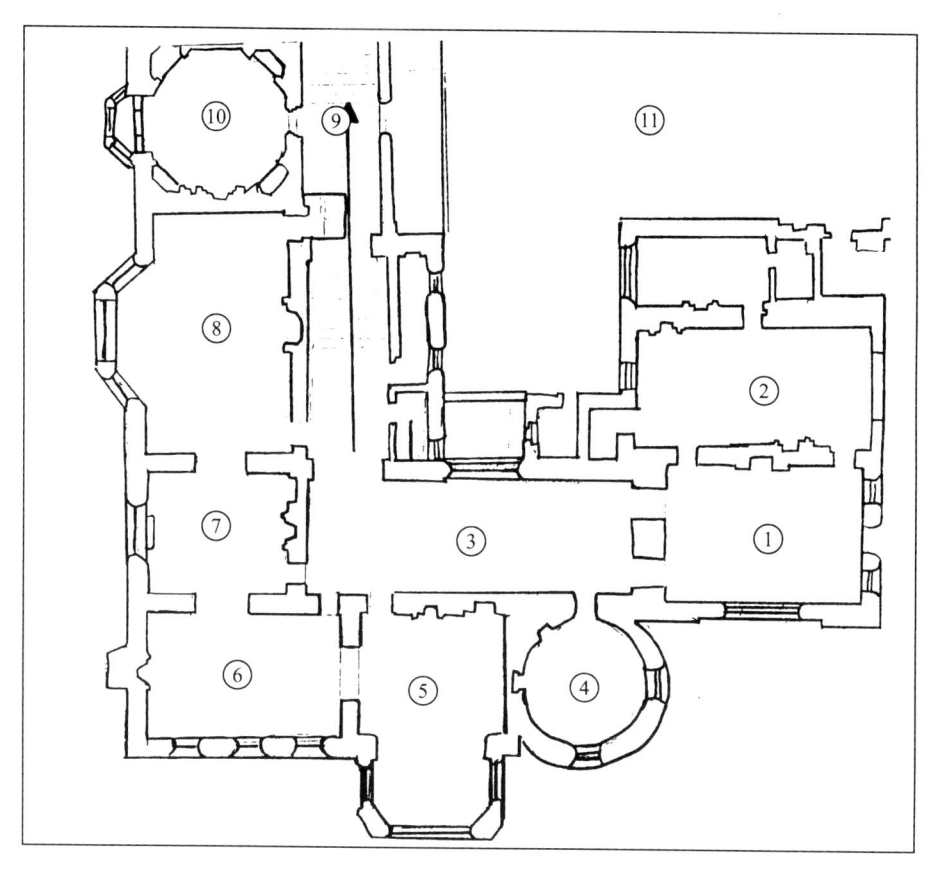

Ground Floor Plan 1909

1. Outer Hall
2. Billiards Room
3. Inner Hall
4. Gothic Tower (Round Study)
5. Library
6. Drawing Room
7. Music Room
8. Dining Room
9. Marble Stairs
10. Breakfast Room
11. Kitchen Court

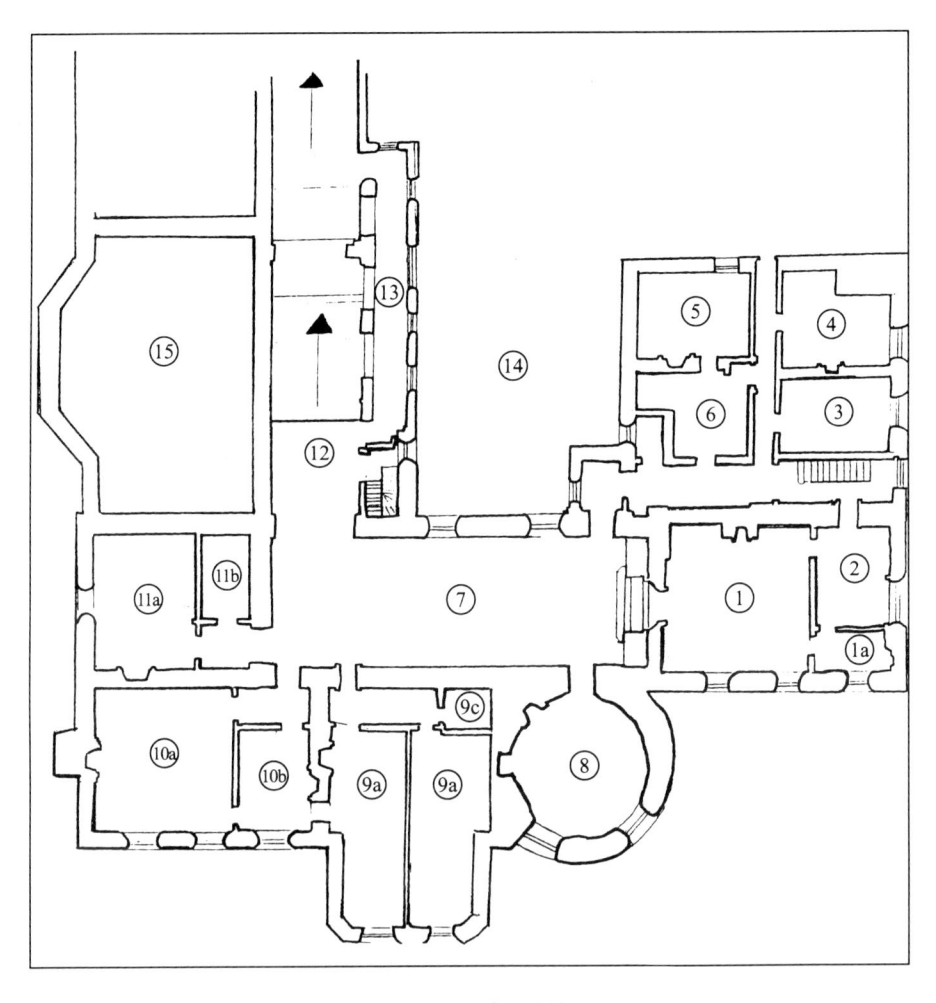

First Floor Plan 1909

1	State Bedroom	10a	North Bedroom
1a	Bathroom	10b	North Boudoir
2	Sitting Room	11a	Rhuddlan Bedroom
3	Red Bedroom	11b	Rhuddlan Boudoir
4	West Tower Bedroom	12	Second Part of Picture Gallery
5	Chintz Dressing Room	13	First Part of Picture Gallery
6	Chintz Bedroom	14	Kitchen Court
7	Picture Gallery	15	Upper Part of Dining Room
8	Gothic Victoria Bedroom		
9a	Octagon Bedroom		
9b	Octagon Bedroom		
9c	Octagon Boudoir		

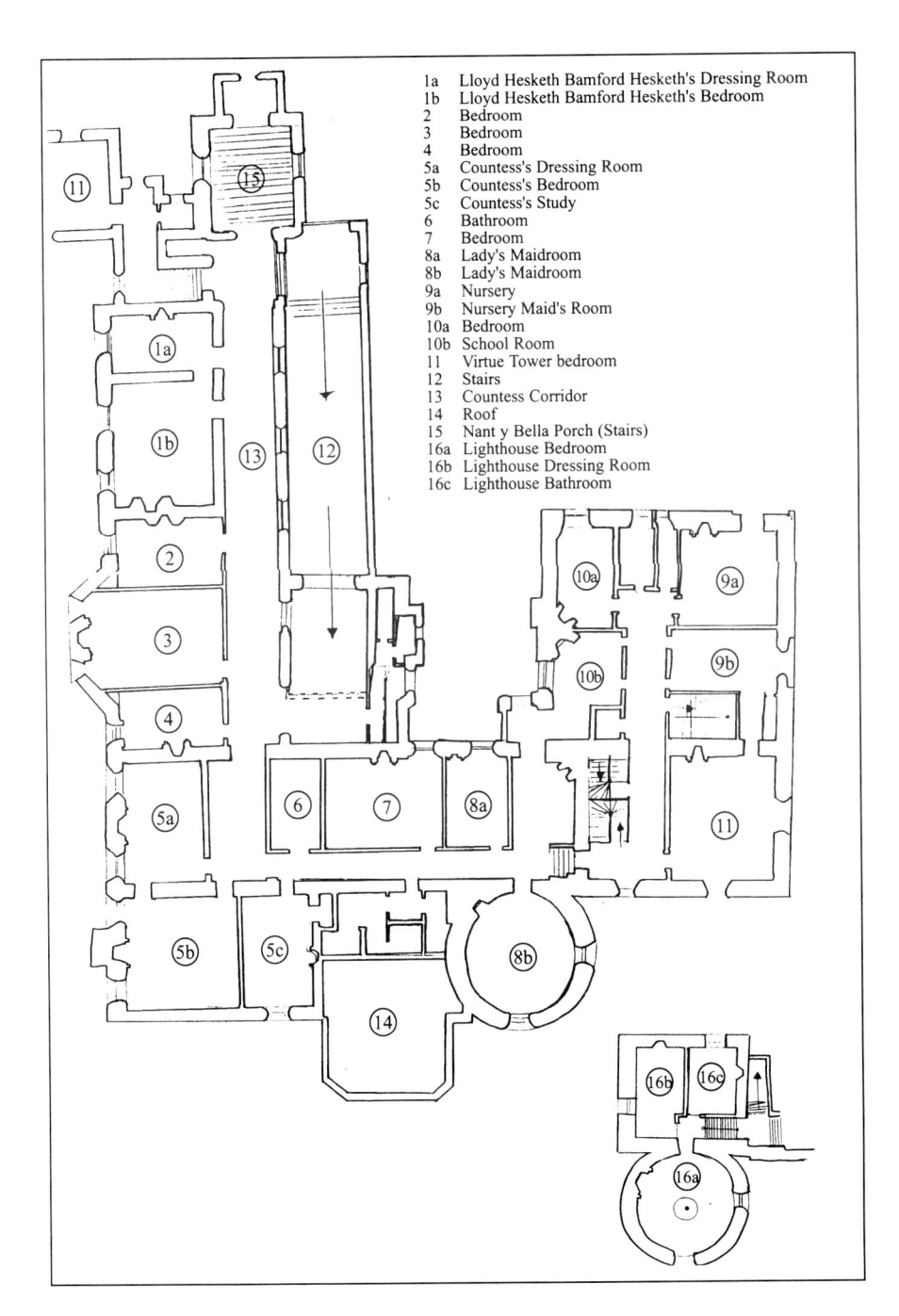

1a   Lloyd Hesketh Bamford Hesketh's Dressing Room
1b   Lloyd Hesketh Bamford Hesketh's Bedroom
2   Bedroom
3   Bedroom
4   Bedroom
5a   Countess's Dressing Room
5b   Countess's Bedroom
5c   Countess's Study
6   Bathroom
7   Bedroom
8a   Lady's Maidroom
8b   Lady's Maidroom
9a   Nursery
9b   Nursery Maid's Room
10a Bedroom
10b School Room
11   Virtue Tower bedroom
12   Stairs
13   Countess Corridor
14   Roof
15   Nant y Bella Porch (Stairs)
16a Lighthouse Bedroom
16b Lighthouse Dressing Room
16c Lighthouse Bathroom

The Second and Third Floor Plans - 1909

Jewish children outside the main entrance of the Castle (Evacuees from Operation Kindertransport) Circa 1939. Courtesy of John Edelnand

Early morning roll call. The Jewish children on the Main West Terrace circa 1939. Courtesy of John Edelnand

In 1927, Douglas, Earl of Dundonald, produced plans for converting the Castle into a Hydro Hotel with swimming pool, two 18-hole golf courses, numerous tennis courts and an entertainment pavilion with houses in the surrounding park. Lady Grizel opposed the plans and dissuaded her father, so they never materialised. The 12th Earl decided that if he could not use the Castle as a hotel, then, it is claimed, no more Dundonalds would live there and so he is thought to have sold all of the antique furniture. That was the last time the Castle was used as a stately home for the family. Nowadays, Lochnell Castle in Argyll is the home of the Earls of Dundonald. During the 1930's Gwrych Castle was left empty and allowed to decay. It is thought that only two old tables and a chair remained in the Castle. The water and electricity supplies were disconnected.

Three hundred Jewish refugees, separated from their families, were housed in the then empty Castle in 1939, which the Government requisitioned from the 13th Earl whose father had died in 1935. Following Kristalnacht on the 9th of November 1938, the British Government decided to allow up to 10,000 unaccompanied Jewish children from Germany, Austria and Czechoslovakia into Great Britain in what was known as 'Operation Kindertransport'. Most of the children could speak a little English but no Welsh, though some of them were keen to learn. The children had a wide age range and the Castle camp was run like a kibbutz. Gwrych remains an important place in the memories of many of the former evacuees. One couple had a baby and another was married. The 3rd of February saw the Fire Brigade extinguish a fire which was started in one of the outbuildings. Some of the children witnessed this but fortunately no one was hurt.

In 1940, six bombs were dropped within the Castle grounds. Fortunately, most fell in the woods and park, but two landed quite close to the Stable Court. Mysteriously, it is claimed that a light was seen in the prominent, elevated Lady Emily's Tower which looks out over the Irish Sea. Could this have been connected with the attack? Did the enemy know of the children's presence in the Castle? These questions will probably remain unanswered.

The children bade farewell to Gwrych when land in Israel became available and they had the chance to go and live there. A few went to America or stayed in Great Britain. I maintain contact with some of these children.

Thomas, Lord Cochrane then succeeded his father and when he received the Castle back from the Government, Thomas decided to sell it in 1945. The Castle and most of the Estate finally left the hands of the Heskeths after nearly 400 years.

John Edelnand aged 15 years in the Hen Wrych nursery gardens within the Castle Grounds, where he worked for a while. Circa 1940 - courtesy of John Edelnand

CHAPTER FOUR
THE TOUR OF THE INTERIOR OF GWRYCH

The tour helps describe the Castle at the beginning of the twentieth century. A reflection of when the Castle was in its prime. Included is a brief summary of contents which were contained in the rooms.

Outer Hall 1950's. Door on the left led to the Billiards Room

OUTER HALL
    The entrance into the building was from the Main West Terrace. Looking at the Main Block, you can see the light, greyish-white limestone cut out of the hillside. A shield was hung over the oak door showing the Arms of Fitton and of Hesketh (centre since removed by vandals). There were two large gothic windows with Elizabethan style iron lattice work on either side. Six quatrefoils pierced the three mullions within the window frames. On entering the Outer Hall you could see the dark grey limestone floor cut into diamond shapes, which was always highly polished. The 17th Century style moulded ceiling with embossed Tudor roses and Fleur de Llys, was gold and cream enriched with red. Two gilted lanterns with coloured glass illuminated the Hall. The two windows guarding the entrance face west and had the initials of Winifred Hesketh and her husband engraved in orange and purple panes. Interestingly, the grand north window bore the Arms of Hesketh and Fitton, portrayed with the family motto 'Virtue et labore'. In Welsh next to them read 'Cadarn ar Cyfribysi' and 'Eryr Eryrod Eryru'.

    Noticeably, this room was encased in a flood of oak panelling which ended at door height. There were two doors, one of which which led off to the Billiards Room on the left and the other on the right led to the Smoke Room. The huge limestone fireplace was in a Welsh vernacular style with Arms of Fitton again, together with the Dundonald Emblem. At three metres high and holding the Countess's initials, Welch designed the fireplace to compliment Lloyd Hesketh Bamford-Hesketh's original ceiling which is dated 1914. It was based on the fireplace in the Great Hall of Plas Mawr, Conwy. Between the Inner and Outer Halls was a central pier with two Arches extending outwards. On the north west wall just to the right of the divide is another oak door leading into the Round Study. Finally, the Outer Hall dimensions were estimated to be 32 feet by 20 feet.

INVENTORY OF THE FURNITURE IN THE OUTER HALL INCLUDED:
Set of six fine old walnut framed chairs.
A mahogany framed settee with three loose hair cushions in repp.
Choice antique mahogany oval wine table.
Finely figured oak octagonal library table with massive bulbous support
and carved lion and claw feet.
Antique mahogany oblong dining table on a carved spiral support and turned ball feet,
4ft 10in by 5ft 6in.
Expensive oak framed easy chairs in hide with loose sowing covers.
Finely carved oak hall cupboard fitted two shelves enclosed by a
pair of panelled doors with panelled sides.
Rosewood stationery cabinet.
Antique pair of magnificent cast iron oblong log boxes with unique floral decoration,
each fitted with two handles and on claw feet.
A Sheraton mahogany fire screen with a wood worked panel.
Choice brassed fender, three fire implements and a pierced brass spark guard.

FLOOR COVERINGS:
Axminster rug.
Fine Persian runners, 13ft by 3ft 6in.
Bokhara rug, 10ft 6in by 5ft 6in.

PICTURES:
Small watercolour drawing in a gilt frame.
An engraving of Gwrych.

The Stone Lounge, facing the Regency Room

THE ROUND STUDY

The Study has been so named since the initial designs of C.A. Busby and of Thomas Rickman in 1817. Standing 18 feet 6 inches in a perfect circle, it had three storeys and a basement. On ground level there were two famous 'perp.g' windows designed for the Castle by Rickman, which can be seen all over Gwrych. Six large mullion divided panels, cut up into sections of three in an arched gothic style with coloured circular glass separating six of the panels. One of the windows faces north and the other west; the Library door faced east and the door into the Inner Hall faced south. The Study had always been the Castle's office, even since Lloyd Hesketh Bamford-Hesketh's time. Interestingly, the large round basement was the Old Servants Hall until this room was divided up in the 1970's.

FURNITURE:
Choice Georgian fall leaf table, fitted with one drawer.
Rare old octagonal shaped mahogany wine cooler on castors.
Travelling clock in a case.
Pair of rare old Adam's single chairs.
Pair of old brass centre electroliers.

FLOOR COVERING:
1. *Fine Persian rug, 9ft by 6ft 9in.*

PICTURES:
Landscape with cattle and hills in the background, by CUYP 1646, 36in by 26in.
Oil painting on panel, of a landscape, by J Stark.

CURTAINS:
1. *Exceptionally fine pair of heavy cream green bordered serge curtains.*

Stone Lounge, facing the West and Round Study

THE LIBRARY (Later called the STONE LOUNGE AND LLEWELYN'S BAR)

The Library was dominated by the huge, considered by some, to be out of place bay windows; early pictures and blue prints reflect this. Stained glass, only apparent at the top, was of a Grecian leaf style, in maroon and purple. The window design was heavily based on Pugin and on Rickman's Church style. Big and airy, looking out over the park, there were four windows. Two windows faced north towards the sea. One faced west onto the beautiful West Terrace and the identical window standing at three metres faced the enchanting east lawn. The shelf below the window led to the oak panelled floor covered with huge Turkish carpets. Interestingly the ceiling, coved at the north and south sides with an enriched gothic oval central cornice, was not painted too brightly because it was thought that the bookcases should be the centre of attention. The classical and gothic mixture bookshelves were immense, taking up three quarters of the wall space in this 31 x 22 feet room. Lloyd Hesketh Bamford-Hesketh could not entirely fill his new library and so he employed a Chester carpenter to make him false book spines. A catchphrase emerged 'Like Heskey's Old Library', meaning something pretentious!

Notably, the fireplace had an arched stone construction, with a type of plaque and an inscription on it (sadly lost). This room had originally no real ceiling light, but Hesketh made sure that there were juts in the walls big enough to hold gothic lanterns. The fireplace was a part of the bookcases and was removed with them, leaving the limestone walls. In later years, the room was starkly bare. Original stone work was revealed because the 12th Earl, in the sale of furniture, sold and ripped out the bookshelves, hence the name 'the Stone Lounge'. In the 1970's it was known as 'Llewelyn's Bar' and was spread out along the western side of the room. A door in the south east corner led into the Inner Hall and the first pair of three mahogany doors in the State Apartments was situated at the eastern exit into the Main Drawing Room.

LIBRARY FURNITURE:
Set of six Chippendale chairs.
Fine quality mahogany framed settee, spring and hair stuffed, in striped silk tapestry with three loose cushions, and loose saving covers.
Four choice divan chairs in mahogany frames, spring and hair stuffed, in striped silk tapestry and a saving cover.
Antique mahogany folding card table.
Pair of fine maple wood reversible fire screens, one side having tapestry panels with the family's Coat of Arms and the reverse mirrored.
Pair of rich coloured fluted mahogany pedestals.
Finely marked Georgian travel clock.
Choice mahogany revolving bookcase.
Chippendale gilt framed wall mirror.
Quantity of games and six photo frames.
Antique pierced steel fender and implements.
Woven fire spark guard.
Choice old marble mantle clock with chime, surrounded by tree carved figures and leaves.
Four small silver candlesticks.
Lacquered circular plant container and contents.

FLOOR COVERING:
Turkish hearth rug in rich colours.
Fine quality old Persian rug, 19ft by 6ft 9in.

CURTAINS:
Four long silk damask draw curtains.

CERAMICS:
1. Georgian teapot, on pillar and claw feet.

DRAWING ROOM
(Later called THE REGENCY LOUNGE AND THE HUNTING LODGE RESTAURANT)

Above the mahogany doors was a mock gothic portcullis, overhanging and covering the arch, enriched again with a décor of rich creams and golds. The three elongated windows seen in the Round Study looked north over the panoramic Vale of Clwyd. A high plaster beamed ceiling illuminated by a huge brass chandelier continued the cream and gold theme.

Traditionally, a heraldic fireplace stood in its splendid white marble up against the east wall. A smaller oak door in the south west corner led into the Inner Hall; the second pair of mahogany doors in the centre of the south wall led into the Music Room. The walls divided by thin oak panels were painted white. Inlays were hung with original Regency style wallpaper, which had stripes of white and cream covered with many pictures; some were even by Rubens and Gainsborough.

DRAWING ROOM FURNITURE:
Fourteen fine Louis gilt arm chairs with sewed wool work seats and backs with saving covers.
Unusually fine carved gilt Louis settee with shaped back upholstered in striped and shot silk tapestry.
Two antique chairs and gilt consul tables, with shaped marble slabs.
A circular maple wood library table on cluster column support.
Maple wood square stool with four cluster column legs upholstered in tapestry.
A mahogany framed fender stool.
Pair of rare old maple wood pole screens with sewed wool work panels depicting the old house.
Two rare French mantle clocks with white marble panels and ormolu mounts,
surmounted by figures of huntsmen and horses.
Exquisite Buhl shaped writing table on four shaped legs with Ormolu mounts fitted three drawers with springs, finely enamelled border, top in inlay and fine shaped green baize panel, 4ft 10in by 2ft 10in.
Two old Buhl envelope card tables, with inlaid decorated enamelled tops.
Maple wood stool in the gothic style with a tapestry seat.
Fine old Buhl envelope plant container inlaid enamelled decoration and ormolu mounts on four cabriole legs.
Choice French gilt mantel clock with sevres panels surmounted by figures of cupids and a sevres vase by Lepante.
Two fine quality antique gilt framed glasses.
Antique Chinese lacquered sword case.
Woven spark guard, steel fender and implements.

PICTURES:
Rubens, oil painting on panel, 'The Judgement', 16in by 26¼in.
Romney, life size portrait of Queen Charlotte, wife of King George III, in Court Dress with ermine wrap, seated.
Allan Ramsay, depicting a life size portrait of King George III, seated in Court Robes with staff.
J Michael Wright, an oil painting. Bust portrait of a lady in a blue dress with green wrap, 29½ by 24in.
T Hudson, portrait of man in blue coat, white stock and ruffle, 29in by 24in.

Music Room - 1950's, leading into the Dining Room

MUSIC ROOM
    This room is my favourite and it was really designed as a vestibule, a waiting room for the Countess's guests, before entering the Banqueting Hall for dinner. The Music Room was also used for exhibitions in the 'Salts' years but became disused after that. It was quite a small room with a huge stained glass window taking up nearly three quarters of the east wall. The walls had the same design as the Drawing Room but were striped red and cream; the red ceiling had a classical cornice, coloured gold and white. Interestingly, the large white marble fireplace was similar to the one in the Drawing Room. Notable features were the heavy Regency door frames with brilliant gold medallions at each corner. They were designed to be in conjunction with the cornice and the dado rail. A bookcase encased in a cove on the west wall continued in the Regency design. The third and last pair of mahogany doors faced south and led into the huge Banqueting Hall. Finally, the entrance from the Music Room to the Banqueting Hall had an unusual gothic wood design, which was probably by Rickman.

MUSIC ROOM FURNITURE:
Pair of French shield shaped pole screens decorated in enamel and gilt with tapestry panels.
Old rosewood banner screen with mahogany support and sewn wool work panel.
Pair of old French ormolu candelabras.
Antique walnut powdering stool.
Chippendale single chair with loose leather seat.
Fine Buhl ebonised and gilt writing table with sunk leather panels.
Fine Buhl ebonised china cabinets 2ft 4in, with ormolu mount and enamelled
plus lacquered doors with Buhl reliefs.
Carved gilt Louis settee with shaped back upholstered in striped and shot silk tapestry.
Fine down cushions in yellow silk tapestry.
Luxurious divan chair in saxe blue tapestry, spring and hair stuffed with loose cushion and saving cover.
Lady's easy chair walnut framed, upholstered in light blue woven silk tapestry, with loose cover.

Chippendale mahogany folding card table, with one drawer.
Fine semi-grand pianoforte in rich burr walnut case by Bluthner.
Rosewood music stand.
Lady's sowing chair ebonised with gilt.
Mahogany square snap top table on centre support.
Pair of brass three-light candelabras.
Maple occasional chair with tapestry seat and back.

CURTAINS:
An exceptionally fine pair of heavy curtains with velvet valances and sewn wool work border.

FLOOR COVERINGS:
Choice shaped green velvet pile carpet, 22ft by 19ft.
Four Axminster hearth rugs, two of which were reversible.

PICTURES:
Watercolour drawing of Queen Victoria in an antique oval, heavy carved gilt wood frame.
Lorraine, oil painting, landscape with cattle and ruins in the background.

Banqueting Hall - 1940's. The door on left led to the Main Kitchen

THE BANQUETING HALL

The magnificent floor of the Banqueting Hall was of turquoise marble, Verde Antico, from Brescia. Occuring in many shades of green, embedded with black and grey veins of minerals. This room was 40 x 22 feet and had a huge bay window looking out over a Venetian balcony which led down to the east lawn.Three huge gothic cast iron windows faced east; and they were supported by two gargantuan Corinthian columns. Painted white and gold, they were embraced with scarlet velvet curtains. An exceptionally fine Turkish bordered carpet covered the marble. There was an unusual mahogany dining table with telescopic extension and eight fine square pillar legs with seven spare leaves, 22 feet 6 inches by 6 feet. A large open fireplace of pure white marble was on the west wall. Either side of the fire was a pair of smaller mahogany doors. Above them were two Corinthian triangular pediments and an enormous two tiered ceiling, richly ornamented in a gothic/classical style.

The first ceiling cornice was a thick stepped gothic creation. Above this was a cove partly filled in with strips of plaster which divided it into rectangles. A second cornice was beautifully decorated with fruits and flowers. The fantastic plaster work provided an impressive feature and was originally lit with a pair of intricate chandeliers. Leaving the Banqueting Hall through the northern mahogany door on the west wall leads you into the Inner Hall; the southern door leads down to the kitchens.

DINING ROOM FURNITURE:
Set of twelve Sheraton mahogany chairs, comprising eight single chairs and four arm chairs.
Half are loose hide seats, the other half have loose seats in tapestry.
Antique mahogany fire screen with tapestry panel in gilt frame.
Three pole screens with sewn wool work panels.
Set of twenty four Sheraton mahogany dining chairs with upholstered seats.
An exceptional mahogany dining table, with telescopic extensions and eight fine square pillar legs with seven spare leaves, when fully extended 22ft 6in by 6ft.
Exquisite pair of mantel electroliers with Italian marble bases and bronze feet with bronze figures in relief. Surmounting three bronze figures supporting five light French brass vases.
Set of four large antique octagonal shaped lacquered boxes with lids.
Six small vases and two jardinieres.
Twelve old china wall plaques.
Twelve more wall plaques.
Two china plated dumb waiters on three claw feet.
Old Chippendale pole screen with fine old tapestry panel decorated in the form of birds and flowers.
Butler's mahogany tray and stand.
Mahogany Sutherland table on castors.
Six choice antique tall-reading lamps with cut glass pillars on square cut glass bases.

FLOOR COVERING:
Turkey bordered carpet, 31ft 6in by 18ft 6in.
Axminster hearth rug.

CUTLERY; CHINA:
Unusually fine porcelain dinner set complete with dessert plates decorated with flowers, having pink border, 225 plates.
Over 600 more pieces.

PAINTINGS:
Sir Godfrey Kneller, life size portrait of the Duke of Ormande in Court Dress, 1685.
Lely, Charles II, seated with long flowing hair and green silk coat.
Van Dyck, oil painting of King Charles I in fully armoured suit. 49½in by 39½in.
Van Dyck, three quarter length portrait of Prince Rupert. Flowing hair, white ruffle, studded pinstaff in ungloved hand, crimson and gold curtain in the background. 47in by 47½in.

Inner Hall - 1950's

INNER HALL

The room continued with the same oak panelling; also the twin gilded lanterns which were enriched with the same coloured glass and ornaments. A large vaulted ceiling extended all the way from the tiered divide from the Outer Hall and at the other end, the old catafalque. This vaulted plaster ceiling had at its centre, floral reliefs and Doric style supports. At 53ft by 17ft with an oak floor, there was another large six-lighter. The window was on the south wall overlooking the Kitchen Court. Recessed radiators were concealed by wooden lattice work. Also built into the north wall was a carved head of the goddess Dana, a Celtic mother goddess from Ireland.

INNER HALL FURNITURE:
Luxurious mahogany framed Chesterfield suite, comprising of a settee and two tub easy chairs in figured silk damask with loose saving covers, each fitted with loose down cushions.
Mahogany occasional table with under shelf.
Three oak book racks, three stationery racks and two table book rests.
Two oblong rosewood writing tables with inset leather top, having understretcher
and fitted with two drawers.
Fine oak cupboard fitted with two shelves and enclosed by a pair of panelled doors, and having panelled sides.
Exquisite Sheraton circular library table fitted with four drawers and on four square castors.
Oak oblong library table fitted with three drawers, on four heavily carved bulbous legs and square terminals with heavily carved lion heads, dated 1680, 8ft 4in by 3ft 6in.
Pollard oak low table on quartet supports.
Fine mahogany circular dining table on massive bulbous pillar and quarter supports.
Chubb's steel safe, fitted with three adjustable shelves, inside measurement, 41½in by 16in.

The Countess on her Wedding Day, in front of Gwrych. (1878)
She was renowned for her youthful beauty in later years.
Courtesy of the Earl of Dundonald

Marble Stairs - 1960's.
Half way up the stairs on the left is the Breakfast Room and on the right the first part of the Picture Gallery

Marble Stairs - 1997
Note the previous magnificence of this once grand staircase in its former majestic condition

Gwrych Castle and Grounds - Postcard, Circa 1980

MILITALIA:
Twenty-eight lacquered mother of pearl Chinese spears with carved steel blades and sheaths, 7ft to 8ft 3in long.
Part set of old English Armour.
Four Chinese and lacquered helmets.
Two steel helmets.
Carved lacquered head forming a Celtic goddess, possibly Dana.

FLOOR COVERING:
Three crimson Axminster runners, 14ft 6in by 3ft.
Two pieces of Axminster carpet.
Four Axminster slip mats.
Three large wood door mats.

CURTAINS:
Pair of exquisite green velvet curtains and ties.

PICTURES:
Pair of colour prints in gilt frames.
Fine old engraving of Sir Watkin Wynn and a small oil painting.
Pencil drawing and six pictures, plus frames.
Ten miscellaneous pictures and sketches.

SUMMARY OF THE BILLIARDS ROOM, SMOKE ROOM, BREAKFAST ROOM, PICTURE GALLERIES AND THE MARBLE STAIRCASE

The last of the state apartments were the Billiards Room and Smoke Room, both off the Outer Hall and close to the main entrance. A significant feature of the Smoke Room was that it had a huge cast iron window which covered the entire height of its west wall, which overlooked the main terrace. Behind this was the Billiards Room. This room contained two pairs of heavy blue repp curtains. There was a full size oak Billiards table, with a set of ivory billiard balls. A handsome fireplace with a marble overmantle was decorated with the Coats of Arms. This fireplace stood south and the windows faced east into the Kitchen Court.

Billiards Room - 1949

BILLIARDS ROOM:
Log box upholstered in plush.
Mahogany framed day bed in repp with cretonne saving cover.
Heavy steel club fender, upholstered in red leather.
Three steel fire implements, spark guard and a waste paper basket.
Mahogany oblong side table, fitted with two drawers.
Folding card table with green baize top.
Full size billiard table in oak, by Orme and Sons Ltd, with thirteen short cuts, two long cues.
Two rests, set of ivory billiard balls, marking board and cue stand.
Walnut cupboard, with two shelves.
Old oak side table, fitted with two drawers, on four turned legs.
Choice bronze ink stand with two ink bottles and two cut glass bottles.
Marble inkstand with two ink bottles and a brass handle.
Choice satinwood oblong table with fluted pillar on tripod supports and a gallery edge.
Blue serge table cover with woo work border.
Fine mahogany dining table on quartet supports with claw feet.
Mahogany portfolio Canterbury.
Plush framed wall mirror.

FLOOR COVERING:
Two Axminster runners, 18ft by 3ft 6ins. Seamed blue Axminster carpet, 14ft 6in by 11ft 6ins.

CURTAINS:
Two pairs of heavy blue repp curtains, ties and valances.

PICTURES:
Oil painting of a harbour scene with a pier in foreground, 54in by 36in.
D Law, watercolour in gilt frame, 'homestead scene'.
Two sea scapes, unsigned, 35in by 50in.

    Leaving this area and heading back eastwards through the Outer and Inner Halls, leads past the base of the gargantuan Marble Staircase which was flanked with gothic ornamental iron work made of brass. The cascade of fifty two marble steps was flanked on either side with an exaggerated dado made of green Verde Antico marble, which was over one metre high. Interestingly, the steps were of Porto Venere, a type of white Italian marble with purple and black striation. The staircase was divided up into two landings. To the left was the doorway of the Dining Hall and to the right was the base of the secondary staircase. As the ceiling continued the ribbed vaulting, the tiled floor represented orange and yellow rhomboids, giving the appearance of being three dimensional. They were superbly made by Mintons of Stoke-on-Trent. The whole of the stairs was illuminated by several cast iron windows and two electric chandeliers, each fitted with twelve lights.

    On the first landing was the Breakfast Room which was on the east side and the entrance to the first part of the Picture Gallery was to the west. The Breakfast Room was created by Lloyd and was originally the Octagon tower. This room faced east and had four gothic arched coves in each corner. The large six lighter window was actually a French window which led down to a venetian balcony. A small marble fireplace was built onto the east wall and to the south was an ante-chamber which contained the service lift from the kitchens. The Breakfast Room was 24 x 20 feet and had a plain corniced ceiling.

    At the top of the staircase there was a large memorial window installed by the Countess, which depicted the Arms of Hesketh and Dundonald. The western first landing had a large two metre high brass gate. In the first part of the Picture Gallery there was a small corridor divided up by three arches which overlooked the stairs. The second part of the Picture Gallery had a wide open high ceilinged view point which looked out over the staircase. A low gothic arch divided the pen galleries from the main Picture Gallery. The Main Gallery was originally the corridor connecting the east wing with the west and was fifty two feet in length. It would have been used just like a long gallery, as in the Tudor and Stuart houses and Palaces. At the eastern end there was a gothic doorway which led into the Rhuddlan room with three 'perp.gs' on the north wall and an unusual window on the east. On the first floor there were ten bedrooms, four bathrooms and three toilets.

STAIRCASE AND THE FIRST, SECOND AND MAIN PICTURE GALLERIES:
STAIRCASE FLOOR COVERINGS:
Axminster stair carpet, crimson, 30 yds by 8ft.

CURTAINS:
Nine pairs of fine heavy velour curtains and ties.

Corridor to the First Picture Gallery. Circa 1920's

FIRST, SECOND AND MAIN PICTURE GALLERIES

FURNITURE:
Two French cabinets, inlaid Tulip and King woods, with heavy gilt mounts. Having choice sevres inlaid panels decorated with birds, fruits and flowers. Fitted two side cupboards with glass doors and centre cupboards with adjustable shelves.
Six cane seat armchairs.
Unique massive mahogany settee with finely carved back and sides, having a loose leather seat and seven loose leather cushions.

Two mahogany hall chairs with carved backs and sides, each with two leather cushions.
Folding card table.
Chippendale mahogany circular table on three square tapering legs and wider rails.
Walnut single chair with needlework back and seat.
Mahogany washstand with gallery back and under back.
Circular snap top table.
Antique Chinese vase.
Sheraton mahogany side table fitted with two drawers on a four fluted legged table.
Fine Chippendale mahogany commode, the lower portion fitted slide and cupboard enclosed by a pair of folding doors, gallery top.
Fine mahogany chest of four long drawers, and two short drawers and a spring drawer.
Two pairs of brass candlesticks.
Pair of metal candlesticks and a carved teakwood tray.
Sheraton mahogany fall-leaf table with four fluted legs, brass terminals and castors, plus two fitted drawers.
Unique massive mahogany settee with finely carved back and sides, having a loose saving leather cover and seven loose cushions.

CURTAINS:
Two pairs of heavy green velvet curtains and ties.

Second Part of Picture Gallery

FLOOR COVERINGS:
Two green Axminster carpets as planned, 21ft by 6ft 6in.
Two green Axminster carpets, to plan, one 9ft by 7ft, the other 14ft by 9ft.
Turkish carpet, 22ft by 17ft.
Hand worked Indian carpet.
Hand made wool rug.
Six ruby coloured wool mats.

PICTURES:
1. *Fourteen portraits of the family and other Aristocrats*

Head of the Stairs - 1949
Note the spectacular six-lighter window. The stained glass was re-fitted by Elcock in 1914.

PRIVATE APARTMENTS

At the head of the staircase was the entrance to the second floor and private apartments. The sharp easterly turn led through an arch into the junction of the Nant-y-Bella porch, Countess Corridor and the Chapel. Romantically, the porch was lit by a lantern similar to the ones in the Entrance Halls leading to the back drive. Nant-y-Bella Drive was the private entrance to the Castle from Abergele and the stone steps were originally covered with more marble. The Castle Chapel, possibly dedicated to Saint Cecilia, was no longer in use when the family worship was transferred to St. Cynbryds in Llanddulas; the old Chapel was lit by a large ornate window which was exceptionally high and faced north. Another window faced south and either side of this were two blocked up windows, all with shutters. The ground level is higher on this drive than the Chapel and so the south facing windows were close to the ground, elevating the room inside.

OAK ROOM
FURNITURE:
12ft massive antique oak sectional bookcase, fitted six cupboards each being enclosed by carved panelled doors surmounted by heavy cornice.
Oak circular table on three heavily turned legs and understretcher.
Ten exquisite needlework panels on velvet.
Two lady's walnut framed easy chairs in tapestry with loose saving covers.
Two walnut framed arm chairs in tapestry.
Set of three Rosewood empire single chairs, with cane seats, ormolu mounts and loose hair cushions.
Small oak occasional table.
Cast iron fender, pair of steel dogs and three implements.
Steel framed fine screen with twisted frame and a woven mesh panel.
Wool work foot rest.
Antique copper two handled jardiniere on oak base.
Mahogany framed arm chair, upholstered in blue plush.
Old oak side table, with heavily carved edge and shaped floral front on carved bulbous legs.
Carved oak enclosed dressing chest, the upper portion having a lift up top fitted for a toilet seat, the under portion having two cupboards enclosed by two panelled doors.
Luxurious mahogany framed settee, spring and hair stuffed, upholstered in cretonne with three chintz covered cushions.
Steel framed coal box on bent iron supports, with iron drop handles.
Japanese lacquer four fold screen, decorated with figures and flowers in relief.
Choice Queen Anne writing table, fitted with three drawers, on cabriole legs and paw feet.

FLOOR COVERING:
Crimson Axminster carpet 24ft 6in by 11ft.

CURTAINS:
Pair of large fine striped crimson lined velvet curtains and canopy.
Smaller pair of the same.

PICTURES:
Oil painting in gilt frame, seascape, unsigned 36in by 50in.
Oil painting, 16th Century, "Crucifixion of St. Peter."

The Countess Corridor contained the Countess's apartments and several bedrooms. Each bedroom faced east; the corridor facing this was galleried, overlooking the Marble Stairs and the first and second parts of the Picture Galleries. At the very end of the corridor in the north east corner was the Countess's Bedroom and Dressing Room. The room had a large bordered Brussels carpet, Queen Anne Mahogany tall boy, Chippendale Mahogany fall-leaf table, inlaid chests and a 5 feet 6 inch mahogany four poster bed. This bedroom was connected to the Lady's Maid's Room by a corridor, directly above the Main Picture Gallery. Her bedroom was on the top floor of the Round Tower, on the north front of the main building.

Interestingly, the Round Tower Room above had a unique glass skylight which was shaped like a lighthouse. It also contained a telescope and tripod made by R Mills of Pentonville. Other notable bedrooms or private rooms were the Chintz bedroom which was close to the Main Picture Gallery; the Victoria Bedroom (used by Queen Victoria on her visit to Gwrych) above the Round Study and the old French Dining Room in the west wing. Another staircase led from the corridor outside the Chintz bedroom up to the top floor and roof.

DOMESTIC OFFICES

They occupied the north and east sides of the Castle below the ground floor at garden level. These were entered from the Kitchen Court and led down to the new servants' hall; four bedrooms for servants led off from here. The hall was stone flagged and had a massive oak dining table. A Butler's sitting room had a wooden block floor with a pair of damask curtains and next to the Housekeeper's bedroom was a pair of crimson repp curtains and an antique oak settee. The Butler's pantry had a mosaic floor, sink with hot and cold taps, an iron combination bedstead and two pairs of brown repp curtains. In the main kitchen was a stone floor and three cooking ranges, numerous copper jelly moulds, fish kettles, coffee grinders, a large amount of tea ware, a 'deal' table with a large marble slab and numerous coco mats with other kitchen utensils.

There were two larders with mahogany topped side tables and a large Kent's knife cleaning machine. A strong room contained a well made meat safe. The electric service lift from the Breakfast Room and Dining Hall was also in the kitchen. A second southern door in the Banqueting Hall went down straight to the kitchen. The scullery had three sinks, all with hot and cold running water. This room contained the Castle's ice boxes and baths. Gwrych had numerous wine cellars and cool rooms. The Boiler room had a large 'ideal' boiler which supplied the central heating. Outbuildings were built in limestone with battlements and towers embellished with heavy oak studded doors to all.

Most of the other outer buildings were situated around the Stable Hill and Court. There was a Workshop, Gas Plant, Electric Light Plant with a paraffin engine by Orape and Gresham Limited and a Dynamo and Battery Room adjoining, complete with batteries. The Laundry was above, with a wash house, four garages and bedrooms. The Bothy could be found at Stable Hill. Practically, the Stable Block provided stabling facilities for six horses. A Saddle Room with four rooms above was used by the servants and stable grooms. The brick built Engine House and Pump House, with water tanks and cess pit were all hidden in the towers and woods behind the Castle. They were still in use until Gwrych was connected up to the mains in the 1970's.

Doris Thornton born in Tan-yr-Ogo Lodge, presenting Mark with the chest which once belonged to Countess Winifred, on BBC1's Countryfile - May 1998

CHAPTER FIVE
MISCELLANEOUS VENTURES

Stable Cafe - 1949, notice the Elizabethan style lattice windows
Courtesy of Stuart Sandem

In 1946, the 13th Earl of Dundonald is believed to have sold Gwrych at auction for £12,000 to Robert Rennie of Whatley Manor in Malmesbury, Wiltshire, who was to be the first in a long line of owners. The grounds were renowned for their immense beauty at this time. Gwrych has always been famed for its gardens and the **"cotoneaster"**, which is related to the rose; this is a rare plant only thought to be native to the Castle and the Great Orme in Llandudno. Rennie who had lived in Bwlchgwyn near Wrexham, sold the Castle in the next year to Stratton House School in Crewe. A proposed development of a girls' boarding school never actually developed into anything and a conversion into a North Wales equivalent of St. Fagan's Folk Museum was suggested in 1948, but it was rejected and forgotten. In October 1948, Mr Leslie T Salts of Hoylake bought the Castle. His nephew Michael Salts remembers the Castle at the time his uncle moved in, with Winifred his wife and their children, Diana and Nigel. Michael's first visit coincided with Guy Fawkes night, along with a superb display of fireworks which were set off near the front of the building. "We were filled with wonder at the Castle itself", he said. Michael and his sister Daphne and their cousins enjoyed life at the Castle. Michael remembers "the impressive Entrance Hall with stained glass windows, a huge stone fireplace with a log fire, suits of Armour and a massive long oak table." There were many fine paintings, some of which belonged to his grandparents. He remembers numerous pieces of antique furniture especially some upholstered chairs in the Inner Hall, which were always roped off. Michael said that a removable stage at the end of the Hall was used by bands or groups to entertain the guests, "But it was the great Marble Staircase, with its plush red carpet, which was the most stunning interior feature. Nigel and I loved to race up and down it – probably to our parents annoyance". Michael moved to Gwrych in 1949 and went to Abergele Grammar School. "In the Music Room was a piano forte (a mechanical piano). We used to pretend to play complex pieces to the amazement of the visitors. The old caretaker Mr Welbourne, who lived on the premises and Mr Frank Kirk, the Catering Manager, were both great friends of mine.", he said. In 1950, Mr Ken Dove came to Gwrych with his miniature diesel train, the 'Belle of New York' and the steam powered 'President Eisenhower'. The U.S. President gave his personal permission to Mr L T Salts to name it after him. This railway went through the wooded hillside of the Blackthorn Covert and its station was next to the top porch entrance to the Castle. Most of the old rusted tracks are still there after nearly fifty years.

On April 23rd 1949, it was reported that an old tree had ignited and then later on the 13th of August, firemen working on the roof of the Castle were watched by hundreds of visitors; the brigades came from Abergele, Rhyl and Colwyn Bay. They were commanded by Deputy Chief Officer D. Wheway Davies. The fire which started on the third floor was under control within half an hour. This fire had been detected shortly after 6pm and was fought by the Castle staff until the arrival of the firemen.

It is claimed that Mr Salts found an interesting canvas in the early fifties, at the back of an old wardrobe! The experts of the time declared that it was one of the finest portraits by Henry Pickersgill and it was then valued at £350; the wardrobe was valued at £7 and the picture was placed on view in the Regency Room. In 1958, the Marquis of Anglesey along with Mr and Mrs Salts opened the 'Disabled Ex-Service Men's Association' at Gwrych, where they raised £200. Around this time various ghost stories started to materialise. Gwrych's most notorious ghost is that of the "red lady", who it is recorded has been seen gliding through the beautiful grounds at dusk. Bruce Woodcock, the famous boxer, claimed he saw the red lady while he was training for the World Title Fight against Lee Savold in 1950. It is said that the "red lady" was sitting in a brilliant long red dress on the terrace overlooking the Irish Sea. Bruce was supposedly taking his evening walk and said he saw the lady weeping. Taken aback he asked, "Anything wrong Miss?". As he approached her she didn't reply. He was said to have been within five feet of her, when she looked up and stared at him, piercing him with her steely blue eyes and then he said she promptly vanished. The "red lady's" identity remains a mystery. Some believe it was the Countess, weeping at her sudden death or perhaps her arranged marriage, or was it possibly some other obscure family member? It is said that the "red lady" died on a fox-hunt, hence her red dress or red riding habit. Others say that the lady was so in love with the Castle that she demanded to be buried there. Was her wish complied with? It may be that because the land is un-consecrated she cannot rest. The road in front of the Castle leading from the Abergele gate has reports of many ghosts, the most prominent of which being that of a witch and a ball of fire which it is rumoured may commemorate the fires of a railway disaster of 1868 which took place nearby. Other unknown ghosts of Lady Emily's Tower are the Cavalier Knight and his lady wife dressed in white, who legend has it, died together at that place. Was the Tower built to remember their death? Apart from the inscription, nothing else is known. The Castle itself had a cursed room with a sealed door which was situated in the old Chapel (gift shop or Oak Room); the room was no less than one hundred and thirty years old. It is also said that the Stables are haunted by the horses which were once its occupiers.

(Castle Choir) Rhyl Ladies Choir with Mr. & Mrs. Salts - Circa 1953
Do you recognise anyone in this group?

Gwrych from the West - Circa 1978

In 1951, the famous boxer Randolph Turpin was said to own shares in the Castle. He trained at Gwrych prior to his victory over Sugar Ray Robinson. Coach loads of enthusiastic fans came from all over the country to see him. People used to wait for buses along the main road in Pensarn and the queues went around to the station itself. The Rhyl Ladies Choir were regular visitors, together with the Abergele Ladies Choir. Singing took place on the East lawn in the Amphitheatre turret. Deck chairs were set out facing the choir and an electric organ was played by Mr Dove. On the main West Terrace was a small café and another gift shop.

The high sloping banks supporting the terrace, housed the children's zoo, which was comprised of monkeys, reptiles and birds. A monkey was then let out to sit in the trees on the terrace. Once a little monkey swooped down and ate a piece of cake which was in a lady's hand! An Indian dragon went missing from the zoo for three weeks and was found dead on some waste ground two hundred yards above the miniature railway. It was assumed that the reptile succumbed in the cold weather. This discovery it is said was made by Harry Swaine and David Jones, both of Peel Street, Abergele, who were walking in the woods behind Gwrych. "The dragon made its escape by pushing off the glass top of the cage. The four foot reptile must have crawled all of the way from the zoo and it must have been exhausted". This was recorded in the Castle records on the 25th November 1950.

Gwrych was also well known for its rented out apartments at this time, Mr and Mrs Dove lived in the rooms which were previously occupied by the Countess. There were three main apartments, two of which were included in the Round Tower. The top flat had a rectangular room with a domed roof and a glass skylight. Mr Salts and Mr Dove welcomed the residential guests by offering swiss rolls and an impromptu concert on a huge organ in the Oak Panelled Hall. Many happy memories remain with those who visited Gwrych during those years.

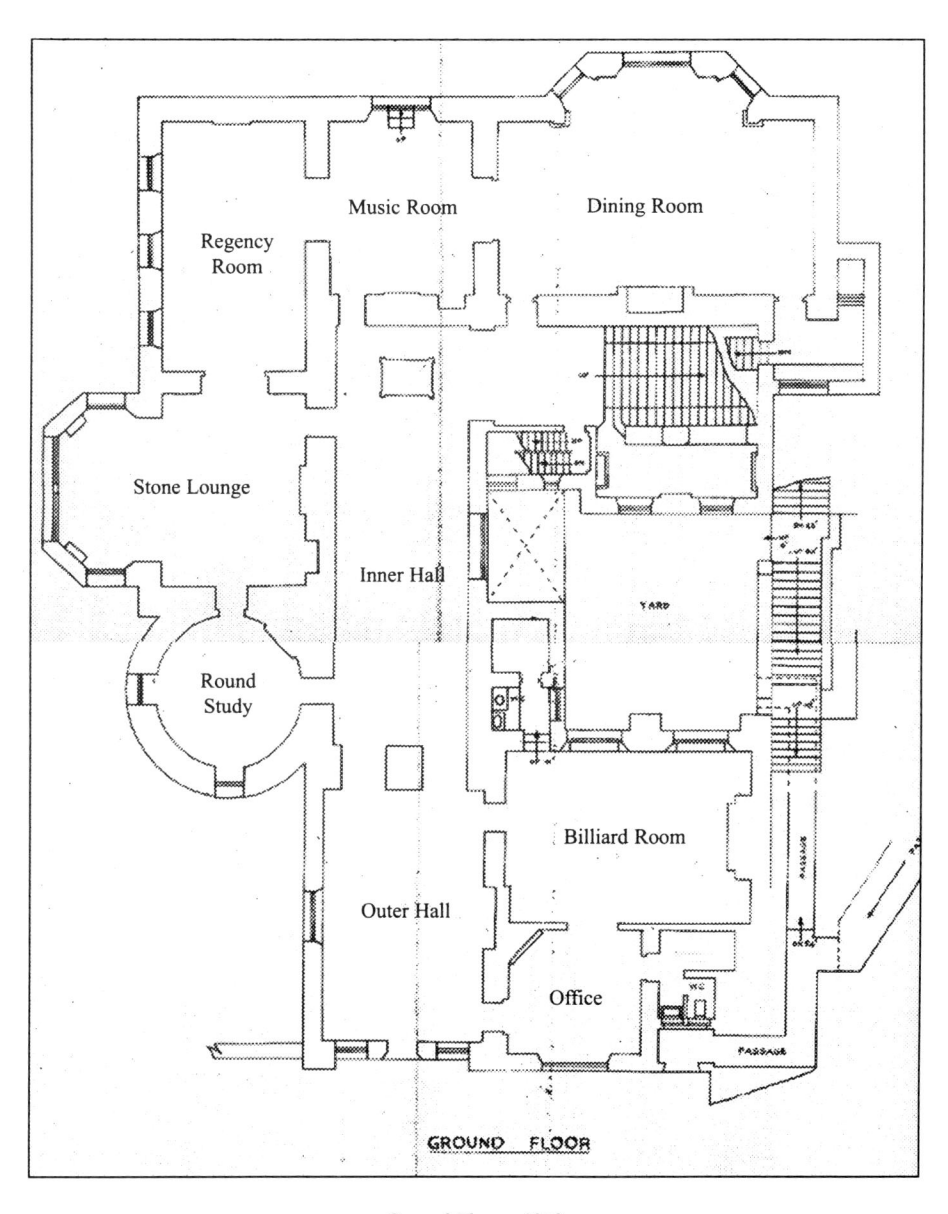

Ground Floor - 1949
by kind permission of the Denbighshire Record Office

In April 1958, there were reports of six fire engines fighting an extensive forest fire behind the Castle. The Firefighters fought the blaze from 4pm until 2am the next day. In 1965, Mr L T Salts made Mr Dove the Manager and then resident Director. Mr Hughes was the Castle's official photographer and his wife is recorded to have had their first child at the Castle, where they lived for six months. In latter years, the Salts introduced a Dolphinarium, vintage car exhibitions etc. and many more events to a busy Gwrych. When Leslie Salts had an idea to link the Castle with a marina at Middlegates, it was turned down.

In 1964, the 14th Earl of Dundonald (who owned the surrounding land) and Mr Salts sought permission for an estimated £5.5 million conversion of Gwrych into a hotel and country club with an adjoining golf course, one thousand houses, a marina and promenade at Pensarn. All of this was rejected by Lady Grizel Hamilton and the Secretary of State in 1966. Sadly that year, it was thought that Randy Turpin had taken his life. It was believed and reported in the local newspaper that he was faced with a £16,000 tax bill, after he went to live on the Isle of Man. Mr Dove it is believed also retired to the Isle of Man.

Part of the West Terrace - Circa 1949

Mr Salts publicly announced in April 1968 that Pleasure Parks Limited had bought the Castle for £100,000.

In May 1970, records reveal that Pleasure Parks Limited were refused planning permission to develop the Castle into a holiday village of two hundred and seventy chalets, with plans for a swimming pool and a miniature railway. The railway, however, was kept and Lady Grizel Hamilton visited the Castle for the last time before she died.

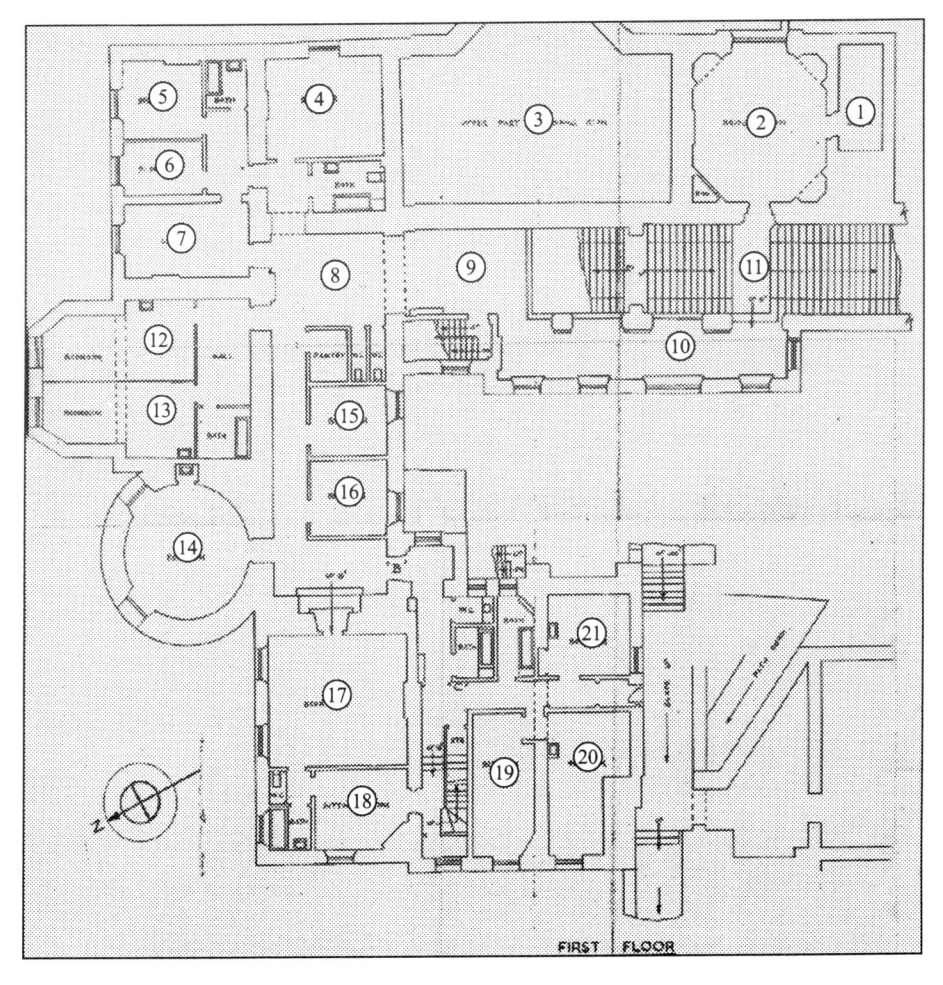

First Floor - 1949
by kind permission of Denbighshire Record Office

Key to the Plan:

1	Muniment Room	11	Marble Staircase
2	Breakfast Room	12	Victoria Bedroom (1)
3	Upper Part of Dining Room	13	Victoria Bedroom (2)
4	Bedroom	14	Bedroom
5	Bedroom	15	Bedroom
6	Bedroom	16	State Bedroom
7	Lounge	17	State Lounge
8	Hall	18	Bedroom
9	Second Part of the Picture Gallery	19	Bedroom
10	First Part of the Picture Gallery	20	Bedroom

Entrance Hall - 1976

Press reports monitored the forthcoming changes and in 1972, it was the turn of Scotia Investments to convene a press conference, when they announced that they had become the new owners of Gwrych and had decided to convert the site of the old east lawn glasshouse into a new jousting court. This materialised and many folk enjoyed the delights of the professional jousters. The jousters occupied the first floor of the Stable Block and set the scene for the popular Medieval Banquets. An array of memorabilia survives from this time including plates, tea-cloths, medallions, etc. Andrew Bown was then the Castle's Catering Manager. The Hall was the focus of the visitors to Gwrych and the Banquets were held there. There were five full courses with wine and mead included. The King sat at the centre and knighted his guests.

In 1975, Darjeeling Investments were supposed to have sold all of their tea plantations to buy Gwrych for an estimated £274,000 and decided to remove much of the previous owner's additions to the interior. "It was 11 p.m. when I had a new idea for the interior. By midnight I had knocked down three walls" said Joe Fleming, then Chairman of Darjeeling. Previously the Castle had a bar, restaurant and various lounges. The bar became the Library, the restaurant the tiered Dining Hall and the lounges the Music Room and Regency Room. Walls were painted with scenes of jousts and hung with metal shields. Joe had a novel idea of converting Gwrych into a holiday club for people who would pay a one-off investment, guaranteeing them holidays at the Castle for the next twenty years, but newspapers reported that the idea was sabotaged by a shareholder who went to the annual meeting to declare Gwrych "as a white elephant!"

Sadly, the reputation of Gwrych had been tainted and unfortunately this would stay with it for many years. Joe tried to regain prestige by setting the Castle for a siege by one thousand enthusiastic members of the Sealed Knot Society of Cavaliers and Round-Heads. This organisation specialised in presenting elaborate and realistic pageants at historic venues throughout Britain. The pageant was the first to be set in Wales. Early in 1976, Chester Estate Agents were offering the Castle on behalf of the mortgagees who wanted £250,000. From newspaper reports many changes took place. Gwrych was bought by Katra Limited, who put the Castle on the market in January 1977. In 1978, Gwrych was bought by Lawncastle Limited, but prior to that, Sweetenhams the Estate Agents said that enquiries had flooded in from all over Britain and one from California. The Californian who was interested, said that he would fly straight over if the negotiations with Lawncastle fell through. Gwrych eventually reopened 'under new management' in the summer of 1978. Lawncastle are believed to have rented out the Castle briefly, but they closed it again in 1980.

Gothic Window situated at the top of The Marble Staircase in 1980

Gola Plan Limited are then thought to have rented Gwrych from Thornwell Finance who had bought it. Mr Ken Wordsworth then rented Gwrych and reopened the Llewelyn Bar and the Hunting Lodge restaurant, which was previously opened in 1973 by Scotia Investments. In 1980, when the Castle was bought by Gola Plan they refurbished the bars and restaurants. The stone fronted bar which housed an open-style cooking area had been designed by the new owners, Mr Keith Lomas, a Cheshire Architect and Mr Richard Timpson, a professional jouster. The décor and furniture were chosen to blend in with Gwrych and catered for up to forty guests who could sit at oak tables on settles and wheel back chairs. The wallpaper was Regency style and attractive moss green curtains hung from the windows; there was a chocolate brown wall to wall carpet. Neo torch lighting and candle lamps at each table added an air of romance and tranquillity. They had an accomplished chef who offered a selection of dishes from huntsman paté to trout and steak. A menu cover portrayed a sportsman enjoying a day's walk in the hills. The fully licensed bar, situated in the Castle's old Library had also been redecorated.

Llewelyn's Bar - 1976

A glowing log fire could be seen and a large wrought iron chandelier, which was placed there by the Salts in the 1950's, lit the room. Large paintings requisitioned from the old tiered Dining Room hung on the walls. During this time major roof repairs were carried out and after the removal of fake panelling in the Hall it was also re-pointed. The walls of the staircase were painted black and the panelling (what was left) was painted a brown and off-beige colour. In 1982, the Castle was bought by a Mrs Donald. Mrs Donald is believed to have sold Gwrych in 1990 to a Californian Property Developer, who with a reported ten million pound boost, wanted to restore Gwrych and build an Opera House on the jousting courts.

The Opera House was to have been dedicated to Richard Burton on the opening night. On the 29th of September 1994, a series of fires were started which attacked the interior of the Castle. Firefighters from all of the local stations rushed to Gwrych after smoke was seen coming from smashed windows. Sadly, part of the floor of the Inner Hall collapsed leaving a twelve foot hole and in September 1995, the services were called to the Castle because the caretaker's caravan was set ablaze, caused by an electrical fault in the connection cable to the Castle which it is believed was rotten. In June the same year, the first floor of Gwrych was set on fire; there were gaping holes in the floor, timberwork and doors which were all damaged. By 1995, the Castle was in a reasonable condition, but in October, New Age Travellers were reported to have arrived at the site claiming to be "guardians "of Gwrych; they were eventually evicted by the Council.

By January 1996, newspapers reported that the Council had put off Castle repairs which were badly needed and in October 1996 severe damage had been done. At this time, Councillor John Pitt of Abergele promoted interest in the Castle, leading to it's re-grading as Grade 1 listed status. Many believe that the Council should have played a more prominent role and perhaps a Compulsory Purchase Order (C.P.O.) might have been a consideration. This would have helped to stop the Castle from falling into further decay. However, if establishing the ownership is in question, this would provide a formidable challenge for the Council to resolve.

Bar Lounge - 1976

Dining Room - 1976

Jouster in front of Gwrych 1976

Gwrych in 1985 - Courtesy of Angela Jackson

CHAPTER SIX
AS I AM

Gwrych Castle - 1993

Present State of the Castle

For the last few years, on most days I pass Gwrych on my way to and from school. The prominence of this Castle and its stupendous charm magnetise many who pass by on the busy A55 expressway. I always think that the Library Bay window reminds me of a smiling face in the wooded hillside, like an old friend welcoming you back home.

From old photographs the area was never so overgrown. Much of the massive structure remains covered in ivy and one of the higher towers has been demolished. Nearly all of the beautiful stained glass has been broken or stolen. Many of the internal heraldic windows have been completely removed. The cast-iron windows are rusting and the smell of rotting wood and plaster lingers in the air. In winter, the rain drips through holes in the neglected roof and then finally into the cellars. Cascades of water come flowing down the ancient hills and flood the Castle. Even in the hottest and driest summer the Castle is still damp. People think that it dries out but it is impossible. There is not a chance since the Castle is no longer weather proofed. The plaster on the ceilings and walls just gets more saturated and might one day collapse with the weight of the water. Whole floors could come crashing down and thus damage the structure of the Castle. It is certainly not safe to enter the building.

This is a dreadful prospect since lay reports have indicated that the Castle is basically solidly built and has withstood it's many "battles", mainly through weathering extremely well. It would be very interesting to have sight of an up to date Structural Survey, as the robust exterior may compensate for the damage caused to the interior.

Outer Hall Fireplace - 1997 (desecrated by graffiti)

Most of the marble fireplaces have been dismantled and stolen. Many of them weighed over one ton. The staircase and 'Countess Corridor' are said to be two of the safer parts of the building: the once grand Marble Staircase of fifty two steps in three flights is now cracked. Cream walls which were painted black are now peeling and the thick stucco is split because of water damage. Floor boards are lifting from their joists and many have probably been burnt as fuel by the 'New Age' Travellers, but they were predominantly rotten and dangerously unsafe to walk on. Importantly, **"No Public Access, Safety and No Entry Notices"** prevail. It is not known whether the roof covering the staircase is secure or if it has yet collapsed. Much of the Corridor of the Countess's Apartment is considered "safe" to walk down **but it is most certainly advisable not to go there**. Along the Corridor and Staircase was the brass scrolled balustrade in an Italian style which has sadly gone, as have the green marble dado that surrounded the show piece of the Castle. Another part of the interior which has been desecrated is the oak panelling. The oak was burnt together with the floor boards and the panelling was one of the last things which was left of Lloyd Hesketh Bamford Hesketh's building. I was saddened to hear of the vernacular fireplace being completely blackened and damaged by the fire in the

Outer Hall; recently, only a few weeks earlier, it was said to have been brightly painted and in good condition. All of the stone paving in the Outer Hall has been lifted. The vaulting in the Inner Hall and Library is still suspended, but for how long? Also the Regency Room has had part of the fireplace and a few floor boards removed, although the ceiling is supposed to be in very good condition and is said to be almost intact. Sadly, the mahogany doors which led into the Music Room have been removed. Half of the wooden floor of the Music Room has now completely collapsed and the window is smashed. The shelving and the other half of the floor are claimed to be dangerously suspended in mid-air over the lower rooms.

Outer Hall - 1997

Deplorably, the gargantuan Dining Room with its huge glassless window is now ripped off its hinges. The fireplace has been taken, along with the green marble floor. All of the ceiling is still intact and the tiered part has not yet collapsed. One of the supporting Corinthian columns has fallen over and it is a gangway across the room, though one of the classical pediments still survives over one of the doors. The green paint is peeling away to reveal the original colours of the Hesketh's Banqueting Hall and the central part of the west wing is unfortunately on the verge of collapse; the floor is covered with debris.

Although the basements are said to be in quite good condition, the tiling and all of the wooden parts of the Castle on the kitchen floors have been lifted and are stacked up in piles. A dumb-waiter which used to serve the Dining Room and Breakfast Room has now been filled with concrete and rubbish. Cellars under the Castle are a maze of tunnels and cubby-holes, all leading deep into the hillside. The Stable Block is in a poor condition; the roof has been dismantled and all of the slates lie smashed. During the filming of the box office hit 'Prince Valiant' they were reused and old hay was strewn over the stalls and ground. (The magnificence of the Castle was captured by the film-makers). Every entrance into the Castle has been blocked up to keep out vandals, but it is not keeping out the rain; three-quarters of the roof has collapsed and this speeds up the deterioration of the building.

As I Am

From an early age, my parents talked about my fascination with British History and Architecture. I am reminded that when I was around four years of age, I asked to visit historic country houses. At every opportunity throughout my formative years, I would ask for historical books on my gift list! My other preoccupation is with drawing and researching historical buildings. Detail and designs are of great importance. I always dream of having an opportunity to study the styles of different Architects and compare their work.

By the age of seven, I had been fortunate to have established an extensive history library, which is my pride and joy. I became very interested in the Tudors and Stuarts, having previously researched this period relentlessly. My choice of a holiday would be to go to the Tower of London or Hampton Court etc. To satisfy my parent's desire for foreign holidays, I would hope that they would take me to locations (like Pompeii or Rome) rich in historical interest! Living in Wales enables me to study the many surrounding Castles in the area and my family support my varied interests and provide opportunities for me to enjoy my leisure time, savouring historical pursuits. Developing a chronic debilitating bone disease at the age of eleven excludes me from sport. This provides me with only one advantage, more space to immerse myself in historical books and reading! Researching Gwrych Castle and its history is an obsession which is both interesting and enjoyable.

My concern is with the neglect to some of Britain's Grade One Listed Buildings. If a building does deteriorate, the local Council or the Heritage bodies have some powers to intervene to stop further damage. Gwrych has been in decline since the late seventies and has gradually worsened with vandalism together with the lack of roof repairs. I started this project because I felt that no-one was collectively doing anything to save the Castle. Together with my love of history and strong sense of determination, I began gathering and collating information on the building's past to create a clear picture of the plight of Gwrych. I made use of the school library, searching through the local history section, then onto the local libraries, national libraries and so on.

From researching old newspapers, Siân Wade who is extremely helpful and is a Reporter with the Abergele Visitor, continues to show the same dedication and interest in the fate of Gwrych as her predecessors. The Record Office and National Library of Wales proved to be potent sources of information. I contacted different organisations, like for example SAVE Britain's Heritage, the Victorian Society, the Georgian Group, the Pugin Society and the Phoenix Trust. Through SAVE I have made many new friends, Emily Cole, Richard Pollard and Deborah who have all supported me during my research into the history of the Castle.

The local newspapers really help by supporting the interests of the Castle. From the first article by Gareth Hughes of the Daily Post who has been most supportive, I came into contact with BBC Radio Wales, Marcher Coast North Wales, BBC Radio 4, BBC Radio 5 Live and HTV Television. In the 1998 SAVE Report, I was very surprisingly described as the 'Valiant Schoolboy Mark Baker'. It was noticed by Maev Kennedy, from the 'Guardian' Newspaper. Following this, I had an opportunity of promoting the Castle on many television programmes like 'The Big Breakfast' (Channel 4), BBC 1's 'Newsround', 'First Edition' and 'Country File' (BBC1). I was asked to do articles for the 'Sunday Telegraph' 'Jewish Chronicle' (Operation Kindertransport) and the 'Reader's Digest'; it attracted many new and former followers of Gwrych. People from all over the world became aware of the plight of the Castle and through this I was privileged to be made the youngest Life Honorary Member of SAVE Britains Heritage; this helped and provided encouragement for me to carry on.

As a result to all of my letter writing and phone calls, I was invited to meet H.R.H. The Prince of Wales. Having arrived an hour early so I could sort out what I was going to show His Royal Highness, I was shaking like a tree in a storm. Prince Charles was terrific, genuine and so interested; it was such a great pleasure to meet him. The Phoenix Trust which the Prince founded, is also very interested in the Castle and its welfare.

Perhaps in the near future, a conclusion to the ownership dispute might lead to the Castle being restored and used again. The Council have done all of the necessary things to secure the Castle from vandals and it is hoped that they might consider all possible ways of erecting a temporary roof on the building to keep out the water which damages the structure.

Breakfast Room looking onto staircase - 1997

Castle Memories Shared

A lot of people have contacted me and I would like to share a few of their memories. Mrs Doris Thornton, born in 1920 at Tan-yr-Ogo gatehouse, can remember Winifred Hesketh the Countess of Dundonald. Doris says that she can remember Winifred leaving her apartments and descending the Marble Staircase in her "Ceremonial Robes." Doris recalls the Countess's Bedroom as being green, white and mauve in colour. Her rooms overlooked the amphitheatre and the Estate which led to the sea shore. Doris can still remember the taste of the delicious tomatoes which were homegrown in the Castle's greenhouses and she recalls her father sweeping the drive. Her mother was a very dear friend of the Countess and was one of her closest staff. Doris left Llanddulas at the age of sixteen, but before she left, she went to the sale of the Castle furniture and bought the Countess's luggage chest. On 19th May 1998, Doris presented me with this irreplaceable chest on BBC1's 'Country File' programme in recognition of the campaign for Gwrych Castle. See page 55.

This was a tremendous and unexpected honour. She is a wonderful lady and I am proud to know her. I am appreciative of the support Doris has given to ASFOG and the precious memories she has shared with me. Commendably, although feeling under the weather, Doris made a round day trip from Oxfordshire in order to support the Castle, at an interview with the BBC in my home.

It has been a great pleasure to meet other local people who have shared their memories. Mrs Roberta Penlington of Llanddulas kindly donated a portrait of the Countess to the Llanddulas Village Hall. Among many other willing enthusiasts, Idris Davies works long and hard in maintaining the current extremely high standards in this memorable Village Hall. I am sure that the Countess would be most proud of their commitment to this worthwhile cause!

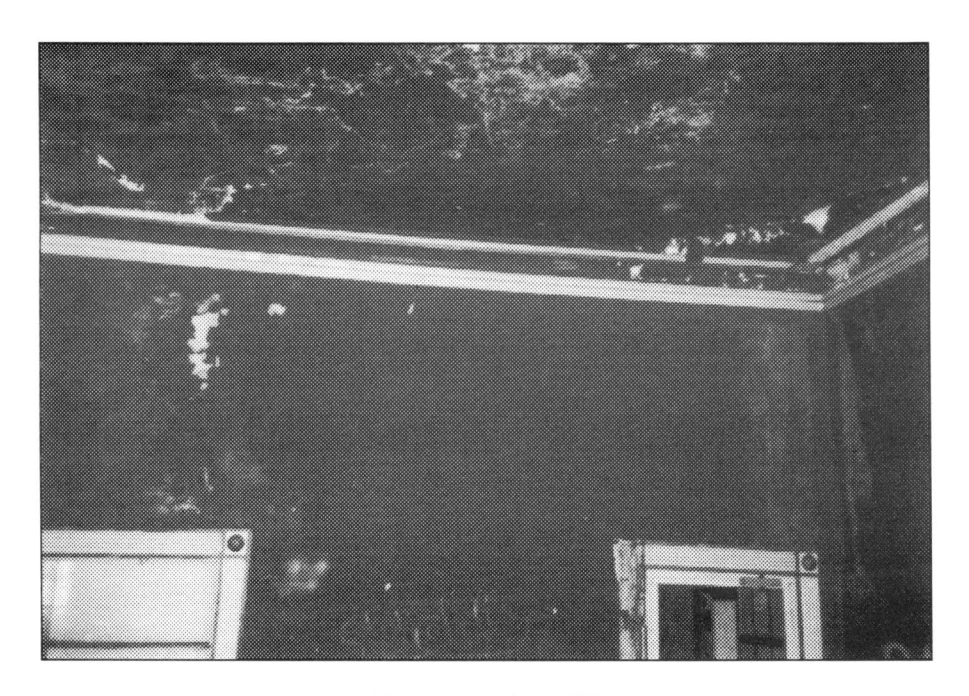

Music Room ceiling - 1997

Mr John Edelnand was one of the Jewish refugees who was at the Castle during World War 2. John was evacuated from Halberstadt, situated in the Hartz mountains in central Germany. He was sent to the Castle with three hundred other Jewish children ranging from fourteen to eighteen years old. Gwrych 'camp' was run like a Kibbutz. An established routine emerged, the children were not only fed and clothed but were thoughtfully looked after. John said that the children had to share everything, even the trips to the local cinema were alternated. He has very happy memories of the Castle. Nostalgically, John remembers Dick Edwards delivering milk and bread to the Castle every morning and also helping Mr Reid at Hen Wrych garden. John last visited Gwrych in 1990 after forty six years. He was appalled by the state of the buildings and gardens, and said they were sadly neglected. I now have regular contact with John, the Jewish Chronicle in London and the MIZRACHI Organisation, including some of the surviving children from Operation Kindertransport.

Peggy Jones, an indigenous resident of Rhyl, shared her own memories in the Daily Post (local newspaper) in January 1998. I contacted Peggy and we struck up a close friendship. In Peggy, I felt as though I had found a 'soul mate'. She spoke with great warmth and genuine passion, her love of Gwrych equated to my own feelings. From discussions with Peggy, one can imagine why so many people remain loyal to the Castle. The impact upon so many is evident and Peggy has a wonderful flair for recalling "life at Gwrych", which helps to bring the Castle back to life.

It was interesting to hear Peggy's account of her youth and the importance of Gwrych upon her teenage years. Peggy had worked in a local cinema in Rhyl (Regal). She was and still is a warm, gregarious and fun-loving character. Recalling her 'courting days', when Peggy spent much time with her then husband to be, Dave, they revelled in the splendour of Gwrych Castle and the spectacular grounds. Peggy particularly fell in love with the Marble Staircase and she has a delightful black and white photograph of Dave and herself standing like King and Queen of Gwrych on the splendid Marble Staircase in 1953, (see page opposite).

The heraldic stained glass windows impressed Peggy. She has never forgotten their beauty, individuality and magnificence. It was Peggy Jones who commissioned her brother-in-law Derek Jones, a talented local Artist, to paint an oil painting of the West Terrace view of Gwrych in the summer of 1998 (see back cover).

Unexpectedly this lovely and immeasurable gift of an unique oil painting was presented to me by Derek, together with his son, who was then the Town Mayor of Rhyl – Mark Jones, in October 1998. Tragically, only one month after this presentation, Derek Jones, who had bravely fought a terminal illness, lost his personal battle and passed away peacefully.

Derek's memories of Gwrych and happy times during his youth were captured in this magnificent work of art. I will cherish this painting and treasure it forever.

Peggy & Dave Jones of Rhyl (Summer 1953). Courting Days enjoyed at the Castle!

Music Room - 1997

Banqueting Hall ceiling - 1997

Ceiling of Nant-y-Bella Porch - 1997

Present Exterior - 1999

CHAPTER SEVEN
THE EXTERIOR IN IT'S PRIME
"Guided Tour" - Walking Route
As it was

West Terrace. (This is believed to be a coach which belonged to the resident New Age Travellers) - 1997

Let's go back in time on a journey to reflect and remember Gwrych before its decline.

MAIN ENTRANCE GATES AND WEST TERRACE
The path this tour takes shows how the Castle used to be and begins on the eastern approach from the Abergele gate. **Imagine** that we are going down the long road until we reach the huge bank in front of the main block. Carry on along the road, westerly, until we arrive at a huge double arched gatehouse. Go through the two arches and up the winding road, noting the old yew trees on either side. On the last bend on your right is the road to Tan-yr-Ogo Lodge. Carry on up to the second bend to find a similar double gatehouse. The huge tower on your right is the ninety three foot Hesketh tower. It is the tallest of all of the eighteen towers and on your left is a two metre high embattled wall which screens the terrace from the road below. The largest terrace is the western one and is divided into two parts; we are standing on the Hesketh terrace which is in the shadow of its namesake tower. We walk towards the terrace wall and look down on to the road below, moving easterly towards the main house, but keeping to the crenellated wall. At a corner of the Hesketh terrace is a small tower which once connected the Castle to the mains electricity. We are now walking towards the south and notice on your left, where a car crashed into the wall, leaving a hole and a pile of rubble on the sloping bank below. Arriving at the narrowest part of the plateau, we now pass into the main West Terrace. The low terrace wall runs all the way to a small round tower, with corbels and crenellations known as the Wind Tower. Built with a higher wall, it shields the people who sit in it from the cold northerly winds. Notice the disappearance of the green and white coping stones from the machicolations on top of the walls.

76

We are now quite close to the main house and can fully appreciate the full force of the southern walls which overlook the terrace. From left to right are the garages, with their two gothic windows. Next, on to stable arch, then the main Stable Block with its solitary round window and several faux arrowslits. Following on is the tower which contained the Saddle Room, an ivy clad curtain wall with a small round tower on its left hand corner, a long high wall with four fake window openings and another arch. Finally, there is a large double gatehouse which is similar to those seen at the main entrance to the terrace.

Main Entrance into the Castle - 1997

NORTH AND WEST FRONTS OF THE MAIN HOUSE

Imagine starting at the ground floor level in the southern corner of the west front. There is an archway which led up into Kitchen Court and down to the servants quarters. Next is a large sixlighter designed by Rickman which once lit the Smoke Room (now filled with breeze block). The main door, guarded by two tall Rickman windows, was once filled with very colourful glass. Above the door is a shield, which shows the Arms of Hesketh and Fitton. Combined corbels above the door show a masonry break, caused when the Countess extended the barbican Entrance Hall. The first floor above the Smoke Room has three windows, actually designed by Lloyd Hesketh Bamford Hesketh, which can be seen in the Stable Block and garages. Across to the left is a window from Rickman's design, which was copied by Welch to fit in with the rest of the Castle. It stands over the Entrance Hall and corbelling. The second floor has two of the Rickman style windows with the one on the right in a recess of two parapets, with corbel supports. A second window is quite plain and is directly above the first floor window. The whole of the top above the second floor is battlemented. Go down the brick steps, past the old generator room and look at the wooden doors from the 1980's. They are also now blocked up by breeze block.

Notably, the north front consists of four main parts: the east wing, Library section, the Round Tower and the west wing. The east wing contains some of the state apartments, which are mostly on ground floor level. Start by standing on the bank, around midway. Look to the main building at the left hand side of the Library bay windows. The basement level has two of Rickman's windows, but were filled with an Elizabethan style glazing, i.e., the criss-crossed fashion. These rooms were originally designated to the Butler. Above these are three tall double cast iron windows which lit the Drawing Room (Regency Room). Directly over these windows are some more of the familiar Rickman windows which we should call perpendicular gothic, perp.g, for short. These lit the Rhuddlan Room and a Hallway. The second floor window is again perp.g., and is above the third window on the right; this gave light to a room in the Countess's apartment.

North Front - 1998

The Library section has a remaining unusual arch with a buttressed base. Inside, under the floor, is an alcove with one blocked up window (probably 19th Century) and another window, unseen anywhere else in the Castle. It is rectangular and is divided up into three mullioned sections formerly containing Elizabethan style glazing. Either side of the walls, on the east and west, are unusual window openings. The huge bay window with two sisters, above the unusual window openings had wooden dressings. There were two smaller windows filled with Elizabethan glazing again, together with wooden dressings above. All three sides have corbelling at the top below the crenellations.

Interestingly, the round tower is next to the basement; the first window faces west and is a double 'perp.g' and adjacent to that (facing north), is another. These ground floor windows lit the Round Study. Two 'perp.g's' above this which face north and two others which face north and west. This room contained the telescope. The large corbelled parapet is battlemented and contains the domed roof with lighthouse skylight. Behind the tower is a large room cornered by four cylindrical towers, corbelled but not crenellated. All of the towers are chimneys. The west wing at basement level is the old generator room and above that is a large sixlighter, once filled with beautiful glass which looked fantastic, complimenting the décor of the Entrance Hall. The window was recessed with corbelling above (like the entrance on the west side). There were three 'perp.g' windows above this and another two above that.

Gothic Four-lighter window in the Entrance Hall - 1999

THE EAST FRONT, AND OUTER BUILDINGS

Leaving the bank in front of the Castle, **imagine** we head north up to the building and go through a small rounded arch and onto the east lawn. Stop and face the sea around two metres from the arch. At the corner of the arch wall is a small corbelled round tower. Walk towards the long low wall before you look over it's side and large buttresses can be seen. Continue along the wall eastwards, until you come to a low semi-circular tower. This was known as the amphitheatre where choirs sang and plays were staged. Notice the flat limestone slabs and the huge crack in it's front which was even there in the 1840's. Carry on walking alongside the wall until you come to a small square turret. When you have taken in the views, **imagine** walking on up until you come into the shadow of the old glasshouse. Only the north wall and foundations of the south wall exist, the north wall had a huge six lighter and a corner tower with one 'perp.g' in the north wall. Carry on past this and continue along again, there is another battlemented wall. At the end below the wall are the gardening sheds, set in a limestone castellated high wall, with a Tudor-arched door at the front which leads down to the drive. Head back the way we've come until you reach the square tower; stop here and look at the spectacular east front. The right side of the Castle at the lower end is where we start next. **Imagine** that we are at basement level near the kitchens and other domestic rooms; the windows are shielded by a two arched colonnade. Across from those are two more 'perp.gs'. The ground floor starts off with a tall chimney which is just corbelled. Up some steps and onto a verandah there was another six lighter and a double 'perp.g' which led into the Banqueting Hall. Although obscured by trees, there was another six lighter and a double 'perp.g', all lighting the Dining Hall. The first floor had only two windows; the right hand one is unusual because it isn't a 'perp.g' and had a red brick overmantle. At the left side is another flight of steps which led up to the French windows of the Breakfast Room; this window is a four lighter. There were eleven windows on the second floor; all were 'perp.g' except for one which is a double. The most northern rooms were the Countess's. **Imagine** heading towards the steps at the left hand side which go up to the Breakfast Room. At the top turn left and you come into a small quad, guarded by a single corbelled turret and a low battlemented wall. A large four lighter faces north and was formerly the old Chapel (later oak room). Go up the long path until you come to the corbelled turret.

East Front from the road below the Castle - 1999

NANT-Y-BELLA DRIVE

This would have been one of the most splendid ways of entering the Castle grounds. With your back facing to the turret, turn southwards and you can see the large 'Conwy flag tower', with its smaller tower overlooking the larger one. Past the 'Conwy flag tower' is a tall wall which is crenellated. At the end of the wall which faces east is another gatehouse, double towered and double gated, it heads into Nant-y-Bella Drive. To the left of the gatehouse is a larger round crenellated turret. A balcony inside the tower leads you down five flights of stairs and there were two ways of going back down to the old jousting court. To the left would have taken you down two staircases and onto the site of the old gatehouse. The second, to the east end of the old formal gardens (jousting terrace) by the means of two more stairwells; the walls continue for about another one hundred feet into the woods, only broken up by several corbelled turrets. Return back to the gatehouse on Nant-y-Bella Drive. **Imagine** heading back to the turret where you originally came to from the east front.

COACH YARD, SOUTH FRONT AND EAST FRONT AT STABLE COURT

Standing at the turret to the right is the east lawn and to the left is another wall, similar to all of the other walls at the Castle, except for an outjut, which contained the Brew House and men's Dining Room. Walking towards the main house, **imagine** we enter the old coach yard. To the right is the Chapel (Oak Room) with it's two bricked up Church style windows and it's large, but short 'perp.g' four lighter, corbelled above to a higher roof line of the building. In a small recess to the left of this is the antechamber window which led into the Oak Room; it is a double 'perp.g' three lighter. Next is the porch of 1845, with its outer entrance which guarded the actual doorway into the house. The higher wall behind the smaller porch, holds in its centre, a dedication by Lloyd to his ancestors. After that is a small low castellated wall which gave light to the Kitchen Court and to the large six lighter at the head of the Marble Stairs. Next is another recess, which with a filled in doorway, originally gave access down to Kitchen Court and the Stable Court. Another double archway, but with a large room above, gives an entrance into the Stable Court. To its left is a part of the domestic building. All of these have small 'perp.g' windows and small corbelled corner turrets as chimneys. To the south are two high square corbelled turrets set up to support the hillside and to serve as a viewing point over the Castle roof. Left of this is a small flight of stone steps which gave entrance to the old Brew House and Dining Room. We enter the Stable Court through the old coach archway and pause to notice the vaulted ceiling. The south range of the Court contains a two storeyed building with two Tudor arched entrance ways which led into some workshops. Above the doors were two pairs of portcullis style overhangs. To the right is a small room which has a small arched doorwell and probably served as a store room for gardening equipment. Directly above the two Tudor arches are the remains of a brass memorial clock, which has sadly disappeared. In the corner of the south block and arch tower is another small corbelled chimney tower. In the centre, above the arch is another 'perp.g' window. To the left of the tower is a wall with blocked up windows and doorways, which gave access into Kitchen Court. The north range has two identical Tudor arched entrance wells, with a similar doorway in it's western end. At both ends of the building there are two small chimney turrets. We now face west and to the southern end are two small towers which hold a staircase which leads up to a walkway. Back on the ground you can see another corner turret which is sited at the corner of the barbican-like structure. The base of the walkway is barrel-vaulted and could have contained dog kennels or something similar.

Stable Court - 1997 (Resident New Age Travellers Caravan)

Kitchen Court - 1999

KITCHEN COURT

To the right of the supposed dog kennels and the north range is the archway which leads down to the Kitchen Court via two perpendicular arches (this part has been blocked off); the wall in between the arches is castellated. Noticeably, the wall of the north range of the Stable Court overshadows the path. It has two of the windows designed by Lloyd. Through the second arch we enter the Main Court. The south wall has several windows and on the left is an entrance into the west wing of the house. To the left is the staircase which used to lead up to the coach tower and it's yard. Down some more steps we reach the ground level of Kitchen Court. The west wall contains on the ground floor the Billiards Room and two more floors. In the centre are some more windows. To the right is a small room on the ground floor which is detached from the building.

Above this is a small vestibule, connecting the Picture Gallery to the west wing A large six lighter was on the ground floor and lit the Inner Hall. Over this are two square headed windows, with a green sandstone lintel. Above these are two more arched windows, similar to the 'perp.gs' and on the third floor there is one rectangular window. The east side is completely taken up by the staircase. At the centre, on the ground floor level, there is a Tudor archway, which leads down to the kitchens. Next to these, on the left are two double 'perp.gs', a six lighter and two windows to the left and one to the right. Another window is hidden from view around the corner. All of these windows are again double 'perp.gs'. In the far north corner is one last window which formed the top window of the original staircase landing.

Stable Hill 1997, stables on the left

STABLE HILL

We leave Stable Court through a tall perpendicular archway, which is corbelled and battlemented. **Imagine** passing under the arch and you can step into a balcony which overlooks the west wing and the terrace below. At the corner of the balcony is a small corbelled square turret. The south end of the Stable Block had a very beautiful window, which lit five stalls in the block; whilst the ground floor of the Stables had three Elizabethan style windows and a lowered Tudor doorway which was large enough for a horse to walk through. The second storey had two Elizabethan windows, which face west. Next, adjoining the Stables is the tower, which had rooms for the Grooms and Coachmen. The first floor of the tower had two windows designed by Lloyd. One faced north and the other east. Directly behind the Castle is the old Bakery Tower and next to that is a semi-circular turret which is corbelled and battlemented. The old Bakery is made out of two main rooms with an oven and a store room. Behind that is another small tower; the largest of all the towers was the water tower, although only the base and corbelling survive. It's high battlements reached nearly two metres. It was demolished in the 1920's, because the Castle had been connected up to the mains.

A wall continues across the hillside until it comes to two square corbelled turrets which join a sham tower which now has breeze block filled windows. A limestone cliff intervenes the walls. Next to the lower part of the Stable Block are the old WC's, leading to a wall which, at its ninety degree corner there is another corbelled round turret. Three faux windows with another corner turret supported another tall archway. Looking onto a pair of small turrets, one at terrace level, which is square and machicolated, the other which is corbelled and round. After that is a low un-castellated wall which ends up at a double gatehouse which opens out onto the Hesketh terrace at which we started the tour. A tower with another faux window and above this to the left was a similar faux window, which has been filled in leaving a thin horizontal arrow slit. The tower holds a shield with the inscription describing the 'Rev John Lloyd of Gwrych, who died in 1775'.

WALKS BEHIND THE CASTLE

The John Lloyd tower contained the ice house. This walk begins in the double gatehouse below the ice house tower (John Lloyd tower). A pointed gothic arch leads you up three flights of stairs. At the head of the second flight is the doorway into the ice house. The third flight takes you up to a path which heads west. Climb some more steps and the paths divide to the west. One path goes to the top of the Hesketh Tower towards Lady Emily's Tower, the other leads to the Bake House Tower.

At the Hesketh Tower, another flight of stairs leads up to the hill behind the Castle and continues all the way around the old Water Tower, the Castle roof viewing point and past the Conwy Flag Tower and down onto the Nant-y-Bella Drive. A second path takes you behind the walls on the hillside and the towers and onto the Bake House Tower. The way down is by the walkway over the old dog kennels and out through the barbican structure in the Stable Court.

Stable Block Exterior - 1997

CHAPTER EIGHT

THE FUTURE: AN EVALUATION AND RESPONSES

As we approach the millennium, I hope that this book will help preserve the precious history of Gwrych Castle and its grounds, so that they are not lost and forgotten forever by future generations. The Rise and Fall of Gwrych Castle is intended to be a durable and permanent history of the Castle. This book describes the development of an extremely complex building programme and highlights the risks of neglecting old buildings. We can only persevere with vigilance and promote constant support for Gwrych, which needs a loving and motivated owner who will carefully restore this extraordinary Regency Mansion in a purposeful way. People continually ask - how did this happen to Gwrych?

On several occasions I have written to The Prime Minister, Tony Blair. I would very much appreciate an opportunity to discuss issues concerning Listed Buildings with him. Perhaps in the next edition of this book, a meeting will have taken place and hopefully those of us concerned about our heritage will receive a positive and encouraging response in relation to this matter. Hopefully, this will be in time to secure the fate of Gwrych and there may be a possibility of much needed change before it is too late!

CONTACT ORGANISATIONS

SAVE Britain's Heritage
77 Cowcross Street. London EC1M 6BP
Tel: 0171 253 3500   Fax: 0171 253 3400

The Phoenix Trust
Park Farm, Gunton Park, Hanworth, Norfolk. NR11 7HL
Tel: 01263 761270   Fax: 01263 768642

Ancient Monuments Society
St.Ann's Vestry Hall, 2 Church Entry, London EC4V 5HB
Tel:0171 236 3934   Fax:0171 329 3677

The Twentieth Century Society
77 Cowcross Street, London EC1M 6EJ
Tel:0171 250 3857   Fax:0171 251 8985

The Landmark Trust
Shottesbrooke, Maidenhead, Berkshire, SL6 3SW
Tel: 01628 825920   Fax: 01628 825417

CADW
Crown Buildings, Cathays Park, Cardiff CF1 3NQ
Tel: 01222 500200   Fax: 01222 826375

Thanks to everyone in the above organisations and those not mentioned, for their support.

Finally, I have compiled a list of thoughts, comments and responses surrounding the Castle's plight. These concerns which are shared by so many people are taken from letters written to the Castle's Society A.S.F.O.G.

Starting off with the Council's response:
"Indeed we share your views about this very important building and an urgent solution is required! ... unless the ownership is resolved, it is unlikely a sale shall go ahead".

CADW:
"We have been in touch with the Local Authority and the Phoenix Trust. We have emphasised our willingness to play our part in finding a solution ... The building certainly warrants an Historic Building Grant towards the cost of repair and restoration. ... Cadw has made clear to the Council the willingness for us to help".

The Phoenix Trust: (Founded by HRH The Prince of Wales)
"It is extremely sad to see the building deteriorate ..... if we become involved with Gwrych Castle at some point in the future, we would like to see you and to review your dossiers of information".

SAVE Britain's Heritage:
"Your campaign to save Gwrych from terminal ruination is an inspiration to us all ... Gwrych is an outstanding building and its current condition is a scandal: such works of art as the Castle should be saved".

Ancient Monuments Society:
"... the power rests with the Local Planning Authority and the Secretary of State for Wales ..... it is ridiculous isn't it that there are no laws to protect Grade One Listed buildings. When the owner shows no interest in their building, the Council 'um and ah' about what should be done. This is definitely the case with Gwrych Castle".

The Georgian Group:
"As ever, the first line of defence for the Castle is the Local Authority who have all of the powers to perform Compulsory Purchase Orders and to serve repair notices".

The Victorian Society:
"If a building is backed by a Company who have the funds to restore it, the Council must immediately pass the building onto them".

The Twentieth Century Society:
"... the current owner is uncooperative with the Council's request for something to be done about the Castle ..."

Nigel Evans, MP, ASFOG Patron:
"As I am sure you are aware, this is now a subject for the National Assembly for Wales and as such is a devolved matter. We may have a better chance of success, if we pursue our concerns from this angle ..."

Mr Richard Glass:
"... That visit to Gwrych Castle triggered off a fascination for Castles, the past and art which has grown to be an important part of who I am ... Too many people now seem to think the world came into existence when they were born and consequently think that history is 'boring' and 'pointless'."

Mrs Rosemary Robinson: (Buckinghamshire)
   "I have been saddened over the years to witness the constant deterioration of this historical building. The Castle has such wonderful potential and deserves to be restored to its former glory. First and foremost a revitalisation programme should be put into action to prevent further dilapidation due to the vagaries of the weather to say the least and to the negligence of the local Council".

Mrs Ivy Eley: (Glan Conwy)
   "I last visited Gwrych sixteen years ago, but I always cast a lingering glimpse towards those 'magical turrets' when we drive past, en route to Colwyn Bay".

Michael Salts: (Cumbria)
   "Gwrych, though not as ancient as some, is still a valuable part of Welsh heritage and ought to be saved and cared for accordingly. Having the privilege of living there, I am disgusted with the current situation and I want Cadw and the Council to use their powers to restore the building".

Mr and Mrs Oates:(Yorkshire)
   "To see the desecration wrought on the premises is extremely disturbing, I hope that you can do something to bring it back to what it was!"

Mr Peter A Rushforth: (Bradford)
   "...I think the Council should find the cash, because it is a national landmark in the same way that Penrhyn and Bodelwyddan are!"

Mrs Elizabeth Fens (Holland):
   "...Such a romantic building, it could be restored and used as a centre for children or even as an exhibition place for the books by Enid Blyton, 'The Famous Five', which are just wonderful"

Mrs Doris Thornton: (Oxfordshire - Born in Tan-yr-Ogo Lodge)
   "I do not wish to see the Castle in the state its in. I just want to remember it the way it was ..... I wrote to the Prince of Wales suggesting it would make a wonderful private home for him and his family".

Although I am too young to understand politics, may I thank all the M.P.'s who have offered support, including the Rt. Hon. William Hague and his wife Ffion, for their interest in the Castle and Welsh Heritage.

From the hundreds of individuals who share my concern, it is believed that this situation should never have been allowed to develop. Perhaps the laws to protect the interests of listed buildings are at fault? I believe that it takes just one determined individual to make a difference. The wealth of support which has been forthcoming to A.S.F.O.G provides much encouragement. Someday soon, we hope to once again walk through those marble halls and take in the rich splendour and majesty of Gwrych Castle.

Mark Baker
   As I am continuing to collate information and photographs, I would be most appreciative to receive any details of your memories.
   For further information please write to: Mark Baker - President / Founder
   A.S.F.O.G. (A Society for the Friends of Gwrych Castle)
   c/o 13 Frances Avenue, Rhyl, Denbighshire, North Wales LL18 2LW

Early in the year 2000, an illustrated book entitled "Picture Postcards of Gwrych Castle" will be printed. This book captures the splendour of the Castle and Grounds in all seasons through the ages.

ACKNOWLEDGMENTS

TO ALL THOSE WHO HAVE INSPIRED, SUPPORTED AND ENCOURAGED ME

HRH The Prince of Wales,
Rt. Hon. William Hague, Leader of the Opposition,
Nigel Evans MP (Patron of ASFOG),
Gareth Thomas MP,
Chris Ruane MP,
Rupert Segar, Presenter BBC1 Country File,
Johnnie Vaughan, Big Breakfast,
Kit Martin, Director Phoenix Trust,
Manon Williams, Phoenix Trust,
Maev Kennedy, Guardian,
Caroline McGee, Daily Telegraph,
Arieh L. Handler and the Mizarchi Federation, London,
Bachad Fellowship, London,
Jewish Chronicle, London,
John Edelnand, Luton,
Harry Thomas,
Bob Ellis,
Chris Keating,
Mike Roberts,
Stuart Sandem,
Earl of Dundonald (thank you for the portrait photographs!),
Denbighshire and Conwy County Councils,
Councillor John Pitt (Patron of ASFOG),
Members of A.S.F.O.G for their valuable memories,
CADW,
North Wales Weekly News,
Rhyl & Prestatyn Journal and Evening Leader,
Gareth Hughes - Daily Post,
Siân Wade - Abergele and St.Asaph Visitor,
Rhyl, Ruthin, Prestatyn and Abergele Libraries,
Beatrice Tunstall,
Rosemary A. Robinson,
National Library Of Wales, Aberystwyth,
Royal Institute of British Architects,
SAVE Britain's Heritage - Richard Pollard, Secretary,
Emily Cole (Commemorative Plaques Historian at English Heritage, London),
Brian Jones,
Doris Thornton,
Peggy & David Jones of Rhyl,
Idris Davies and The Llanddulas Village Hall supporters,
Roberta and Frank Penlington
Staff and Pupils of Rydal Penrhos School, Colwyn Bay,

With thanks to my family and friends who always support me in everything that I do.